Praise for *Micro Practices for Justice Ministry*

Approaching how pastors sustain the hard work of justice ministry through the "little things" they do to connect with others and remain faithful to their call gives us a rich resource for our own ministries. Sample does it again—getting to the heart of what can sustain us while encouraging us to take bolder steps to help bring in the new heaven and new earth.

Emilie M. Townes
E. Rhodes and Leona B. Carpenter University Professor of Womanist Ethics and Society and Gender and Sexuality Studies
Vanderbilt University Divinity School

Nothing Tex Sample ever does leaves you feeling settled. This is particularly true of his writing, which always pokes, prods, and stops you in your tracks. Tex makes you really think and feel and, maybe most important, act. *Micro Practices for Justice Ministry* does all this and more. In this book, Tex interviews an amazingly diverse array of justice practitioners in an effort to uncover how they do what they do. "Little things" is the refrain throughout and vignette by vignette you begin to say to yourself, "I can do this! This inspires me to wage justice in the world." Tex helps you understand what it means to be a partner with God in God's good work. Read this, and then go and do likewise.

Paul Wesley Chilcote
Director of the Centre for Global Wesleyan Theology
at Wesley House, Cambridge, UK

If you are looking for an antidote for cynicism or despair about the state of the contemporary church, this book is for you. Without any hint of romanticism or sentimentalism, Sample wittily, wisely, and judiciously collects and narrates the work of profound witnesses, showing us how small things make for significant changes. The fruit of his years of work in ministry settings, attention to oral cultures, and a testimony to his love for Jesus, this is a splendid work that should be read by anyone who knows the church is in a mess right now and seeks a faithful way to the other side.

D. Stephen Long
Cary M. Maguire University Professor of Ethics
Southern Methodist University

Tex Sample, well-known theological professor and author, has consistently integrated scholarship with community involvement and justice ministry. In this remarkable book, Sample reports on interviews with dozens of men and women who, like him, are engaged in justice ministry. Anyone sharing in this calling will find these candid responses a vital help in developing spiritual, theologically based and pragmatic practices that inform and help to sustain faithful ministry in the public sphere.

Neal Fisher
Retired President of Garrett-Evangelical Theological Seminary

For any who consider practicing justice as integral to Christian discipleship and ministry, this book is a vast storehouse of insight and inspiration. Through analysis gleaned from attentive listening to diverse and creative practitioners of justice, Tex Sample has gifted us with an invaluable, practical resource for doing justice in these turbulent and polarized times.

Bishop Kenneth L. Carder
Ruth W. and A. Morris Williams Distinguished Professor Emeritus
of the Practice of Christian Ministry
Duke Divinity School

MICRO PRACTICES FOR JUSTICE MINISTRY

MICRO PRACTICES FOR JUSTICE MINISTRY

DOING LITTLE THINGS FOR THE COMMON GOOD

TEX SAMPLE

Micro Practices for Justice Ministry: Doing Little Things for the Common Good

At the time of publication, all websites referenced in this book were valid. However, due to the fluid nature of the Internet, some addresses may have changed, or the content may no longer be relevant.

Cover design: Faceout Studios
Interior design and typesetting: PerfecType | Nashville, TN

ISBN: 978-0-8358-2053-0
Epub ISBN: 978-0-8358-2054-7

CONTENTS

ACKNOWLEDGMENTS

When I write a book, what I feel most is a sense of indebtedness. I count the promissory notes to my parents and my teachers, to the scholarship that has shaped me, to the schools and institutions that opened the world, to the friendships that have sustained me with loyalty and affection, to the church that has been my touchstone through thick and thin, and to an Incarnate God whose reach is beyond the stars and whose intimacy is close enough to goose you.

All of that is true with this text, but I have been pleasantly surprised to also receive a massive gift from this work: the witness I received from the pastors I interviewed. I began this project with a clear sense that the clergy who do justice ministry know how to do many small, face-to-face, group practices very well. I had seen this happen on many occasions across the years, so this was no surprise. What I had not expected was that I would be so moved, so stirred by their reports. They were not merely research subjects whose work I explored, but evangels whose testimony came alive and touched and changed me.

I have been involved in justice work myself almost all my adult life, but I have been informed and influenced in this research and writing in ways I never anticipated. It is strange, indeed, to live in a world of practices and then to have that scope of action opened in so many ways that you feel like an alien in a festivity of hospitality.

So, this is an expression of appreciation for those who got me to the party and for those who made it such a celebration. First, I thank the organizers and others who helped me find many of the clergy I interviewed. I think here alphabetically of Gayle Briscoe, Kenneth Carder, Ernie Cortés, Michael Enriquez, David Gerth, Joel N. Martinez, Lora McDonald, Jorge Montiel, Joe Rubio, and Paul Turner.

Of course, I thank the clergy who accepted my invitation for an interview. I knew they were busy people, but I learned more about how engaged they were in my attempts to find times for interviews, to do follow-up questions, and to check the accuracy of what I quoted from them. The scheduled nature of their lives and the commitment required to live out that kind of dedication only deepened my debt and my gratitude.

I am deeply indebted to Rev. Pamela D. Couture, who serves as the Jane and Geoffrey Martin Chair in Church and Community at Emmanuel College of Victoria University. Her careful editing of my early draft of this manuscript—using her eye for punctuation, for clarity of communication, and for meaning through elaboration—is highly appreciated. I am also grateful to Lauren Arieux Bryan who did a final reading of the manuscript, making a significant contribution to its clarity. Errors that remain are clearly mine.

I am grateful for David Teel, a previous editor of mine on two books. He led me to Upper Room Books and to Michael Stephens, my editor for this volume. I am delighted and blessed by this new relationship with The Upper Room and by Michael's careful assistance and thoughtful guidance, and I look forward to conversations with a new set of friends through Upper Room Books.

My wife, Peggy, and I have engaged in micro practices as an ongoing part of our lives together. We have rituals that occur many times each day such as kissing and repeating liturgies of professing our love for each other. My favorite, a litany I really like, is "You and Jesus are the best two things that ever happened to me."

CLERGY BIOGRAPHIES

Doug Alpert

Rabbi Doug Alpert is the spiritual leader of Congregation Kol Ami in Kansas City, Missouri. Before he began his rabbinic studies, he was a lawyer and served as the executive director of the Kansas City Jazz Commission and legal counsel for the International Association of Jazz Educators. Active in local and national Jewish communities, he serves in nearly two dozen social justice organizations, holding numerous leadership positions.

Karen Anderson

Rev. Karen Anderson is Senior Pastor of First AME Church in Las Vegas, Nevada. Previously, she pastored Ward Chapel AME Church in Florissant, Missouri. She holds leadership at various levels of the AME Church and within the community. In Florissant she was board president for Gamaliel's Metropolitan Congregations United (MCU), board member of Magdalene St. Louis, and a cabinet member of Interfaith Partnership and Flourish St. Louis. She co-chaired

Hazelwood School District's Clergy Coalition and is co-founder of "The Mother's March" and "When Women Gather."

Stanley E. Basler

Rev. Stanley E. Basler, an ordained elder in The United Methodist Church, has served as both a pastor and in an Annual Conference position in restorative justice in Oklahoma. He is a specialist in prison ministry and holds degrees in law and in theology.

Traci Blackmon

Rev. Traci Blackmon was pastor of Christ the King United Church of Christ in Florissant, Missouri, on August 9, 2014, when police officer Darren Wilson shot and killed Michael Brown, an unarmed Black teenager. She is the CEO and founder of HopeBuilds, LLC, a consultancy for communities, corporations, and congregations eager to build the just and equitable world they imagine. She also serves as chaplain for the Central Region of Alpha Kappa Alpha Sorority, Inc.

Bill Breeden

Rev. Bill Breeden is a Unitarian Universalist minister who was raised in the holiness tradition and at one time ordained in the Church of the Nazarene. He has served Christian churches as pastor and consorted with people like Philip Berrigan and Kurt Vonnegut. Howard Zinn included him in his *People's History of the United States* as the only person to serve time because of the Iran/Contra scandal. He made two trips to Nicaragua during the Contra wars and once spent four days in a Honduran military prison.

Emanuel Cleaver II

Rev. Emanuel Cleaver II is the congressman representing Missouri's Fifth Congressional District, serving his tenth term. Previously elected for twelve years on the city council of Kansas City, Cleaver became the city's first African American mayor in 1991. Through his political work, he has brought major corporations to the city, led the effort to build the South Midtown Roadway, and has been a force in the 18th and Vine redevelopment. He was a key player in the establishment of a Family Division of the Municipal Court and the reconstruction and beautification of Brush Creek in the city. Cleaver was the pastor of the St. James UMC in Kansas City, Missouri, from 1972 to 2009.

Erin Counihan

Rev. Erin Counihan is pastor of the Church of the Pilgrims in Washington, DC. Previously she was pastor at Oak Hill Presbyterian Church in St. Louis, Missouri. She has a B.A. in Politics and Government from Ohio Wesleyan University, an M.Div. from Princeton Theological Seminary, and is currently working on her Doctor of Ministry at Eden Theological Seminary. She has served several roles in presbytery and community leadership and is a frequent conference workshop leader and preacher.

John W. Culp

Rev. John W. Culp is a retired pastor in the South Carolina Conference of The United Methodist Church, having served churches there for forty-five years. Culp organized the Salkehatchie Summer Service program in which church members, especially youth, go into impoverished areas throughout South Carolina to make home improvements. He is also the founder of Asbury Missioners, a ministry to teenagers whose parents are alcoholics or otherwise addicted. He is a constant source of mercy and justice innovations and a continual gadfly in the church and the larger community.

Joseph W. Daniels Jr.

Rev. Joseph W. Daniels Jr. serves as lead pastor at Emory UMC in Washington, DC. He is very active in community affairs, having served as a co-chair of the Washington Interfaith Network (WIN) as well as on the board of directors of the STEP Foundation and Ephesians Life Ministries. He teaches at Wesley Theological Seminary and has provided mission service to churches in Zimbabwe and South Africa, where he offers training in community development. His published books are *Begging for REAL Church* (2009), *The Power of REAL* (2011), and *Walking with Nehemiah* (2014). He is a Rockefeller Next Generation Leadership Fellow.

Harriet Dennis

Rev. Harriet Dennis is founder and executive director of Issues of Life International Ministries, in Baltimore Maryland. They have begun a church planting initiative in Colorado Springs, Colorado, and currently work internationally with churches in Kenya and Tanzania.

Nancy Dennis

Rev. Nancy Dennis is pastor of Saint Stephen's AME Church in Unionville, Easton, Maryland. She is a leader in BRIDGE Maryland,

Inc., a faith-based 501(c)(3) that organizes communities throughout the state of Maryland with offices in Baltimore. Together, faith communities build power to pursue equity and opportunity for all Marylanders. Bridge is an active affiliate of the Gamaliel Network.

Renae Extrum-Fernandez

Rev. Renae Extrum-Fernandez has worked in church and community outreach in Fresno, California, as part of the United Methodist US-2 program. After seminary she served La Iglesia Metodista Unida Central in San Francisco for five years, then Palo Alto UMC for four years as associate pastor. Next, she pastored Lake Merritt UMC for five years, and then Walnut Creek UMC for nine years as lead pastor. She was also appointed a district superintendent of the Bayview District and later the Bridges District.

John Flowers

Rev. John Flowers is a teacher, mentor, and coach for congregations. He is an ordained United Methodist pastor with years of experience in congregational ministry. For years he was pastor of Travis Park UMC in San Antonio, Texas.

Harold W. Garman

Rev. Harold W. Garman has served as the executive director of the Inner-City Parish in Kansas City, Missouri, as executive director of Priority One of Greater Syracuse, New York, dealing with racism and related issues, and as executive director of the Syracuse Metropolitan Commission of The United Methodist Church, while also pastoring the Oran Community Church. In the eighties and nineties he was first the pastor of Bellevue Heights United Methodist Church and then senior pastor of the University United Methodist Church, both in Syracuse, New York. In "retirement" since 1998, he has been actively organizing interfaith and interdenominational efforts for racial justice with a project to reduce youth violence and has served as a consultant to the Urban Ministry Program at Wesley Theological Seminary in Washington, DC. Since moving to Gaithersburg, Maryland, he has organized Gaithersburg Beloved Community Initiative as a way of developing relationships between residents of Asbury Methodist Village and people living in the area, a locale with a high instance of poverty and a large Latino population.

Robert Lee Hill

Rev. Robert Lee Hill was pastor of Community Christian Church in Kansas City for thirty years. He now serves as a community consultant, most recently for the Kauffman Foundation in Kansas City. He has been active in community organizing in the city and is an activist for a wide range of social issues.

Gabrielle Kennedy

Rev. Gabrielle Kennedy is pastor of Buren Chapel AME Church in Herculaneum, Missouri, where she is also director of Faith and For the Sake of All, a nonprofit that works with faith communities concerned with racial disparities in health and other life outcomes. She is also an African American parent in the Lindbergh School District and a member of LEAD (Lindbergh Equity and Diversity), a group of mostly White parents who want to encourage the district to adopt anti-racism practices.

Edwin King Jr.

Rev. Edwin King Jr. played an important role in the civil rights movement of the sixties as a member of the Fellowship of Reconciliation in protests in Alabama, as chaplain at Tougaloo College, in the Mississippi Summer Project of 1964, as a cofounder of the Mississippi Freedom Democratic party, and as a delegate to three Democratic National Conventions. In the latter part of his career, he served on the faculty of University of Mississippi Medical Center, School of Health Related Professions, faculty in sociology and in ethics. A brief but good account of his life and contributions can be found on Wikipedia under the title "Ed King (activist)."

William H. Lamar IV

Rev. William H. Lamar IV is pastor of Metropolitan AME Church in Washington, DC. Ordained as an itinerant elder in 2000 at the Florida Annual Conference of the AME Church, Lamar has also served congregations in Monticello, Florida; Orlando, Florida; Jacksonville, Florida; and Hyattsville, Maryland.

Sam Mann

Rev. Sam Mann is the Pastor Emeritus of Saint Mark Union Church, a core city congregation in the Black community in Kansas City, Missouri, having previously served for forty-four years as pastor/

administrator of the Church and of United Inner-City Services, a social services agency. An activist, often arrested, he once led a protest of the meeting of a national corporation in Kansas City, at which he kicked in the door after it was locked to keep out demonstrators.

Joel N. Martinez

Bishop Joel N. Martinez is a retired bishop of The United Methodist Church, having served from 1992 to 2008. His pastoral appointments were in Dallas, San Antonio, and El Paso. He served as director of Planning and Development at Newark Houchen Center in El Paso and later, as executive secretary of the Office of Ethnic and Language Ministries, National Division, General Board of Global Ministries. His ministry also included an appointment as a district superintendent in the Rio Grande Conference and as president of the Greater Dallas Community of Churches. He was a delegate to the Seventh Assembly of the World Council of Churches in Canberra, Australia, 1991. He now co-chairs the national board of the Industrial Areas Foundation.

Angelique Mason

Rev. Angelique Mason is the pastor of Allen AME Church in Hillsboro, Maryland. Previously she served as pastor to the historic Holy Trinity African Methodist Episcopal Church in Edesville, Maryland (2007–2011). An itinerant in the African Methodist Episcopal Church, she is co-president of BRIDGE Maryland, Inc. and a member of the NAACP.

R. Mark Matheny

Rev. Mark Matheny of the Tennessee-Western Kentucky Conference served for forty-two years in urban ministry in Memphis, Tennessee. This includes leading a variety of local churches, a campus ministry, Metro Mission work, and executive directorship of United Methodist Neighborhood Centers of Memphis. Matheny also served as a district superintendent and was founder of several nonprofit ministries, including the Soul Force Initiative for fostering non-violence.

Ingrid McIntyre

Rev. Ingrid McIntyre is executive director and cofounder of the homeless advocacy organization Open Table Nashville and founder/developer of the Village at Glencliff, a medical respite for the unhomed community. She also serves as pastor at Glencliff UMC in Nashville, Tennessee.

Holly McKissick

Rev. Holly McKissick is the founding pastor of Peace Church UCC (established in 2011) in Kansas City, Missouri. A contributing religion writer for the *Kansas City Star,* she is the author of *Tall Poppy: How to Lead Without Losing Your Head* (2013). A longtime community activist and spirited voice for progressive causes, McKissick is a mentor at Operation Breakthrough, Big Brothers, Big Sisters and Lead to Read. She is active in broad-based community organizing with StandUp KC, Missouri Jobs with Justice, and the Metro Organization for Racial and Economic Equity.

David W. Meredith

Rev. David W. Meredith, a United Methodist elder, is pastor of Clifton UMC in Cincinnati, Ohio, and director of Urban Ministry for the Ohio River Valley District, where he works with seven urban locations in Cincinnati, Hamilton, and Middletown. From 1993 to 1997, he was executive director of Inter Parish Ministry on the east side of Hamilton County, Ohio. In that capacity, he helped launch two freedom schools and expansive partnerships between congregations in many denominations, civic organizations, and businesses.

David Carl Olson

Rev. David Carl Olson is Associate Minister for Congregational Life at the Unitarian Universalist Congregation at Shelter Rock in Manhasset, New York. Previously he served as minister of the First Unitarian Church of Baltimore, Maryland (2009–2022), minister of The Unitarian Universalist Congregation of Flint Michigan (2005–2009), minister of the Community Church of Boston, Massachusetts (1998–2005), and Sunday Service Facilitator at the Community Church of Boston, Massachusetts (1996–1998).

Jose L. Palos

Rev. Jose L. Palos served Methodist and then United Methodist churches in the Rio Grande Conference in Texas. He was actively involved in the COPS METRO community organizing effort in San Antonio when he was pastor of La Trinidad UMC (2002–2006) and El Divino Salvador UMC (2006–2011). In addition to serving as a pastor, he was the Conference Council Director (1980–1986),

Commissioned Conference Coordinator of Congregational Development (1986–1993), and Coordinator of the National Plan for Hispanic/Latino Ministry of the UMC, New York City (1993–2002).

Cody J. Sanders

Rev. Cody J. Sanders is pastor of the Old Cambridge Baptist Church in Cambridge Massachusetts. He is also the American Baptist chaplain at Harvard University and serves in that capacity as adviser for LGBTQ+ Affairs in the Office of Religious, Spiritual, and Ethical Life at the Massachusetts Institute of Technology. An active scholar, he teaches at several theological schools and is an author.

Marti Scott

Rev. Marti Scott was ordained as an elder in the Northern Illinois Conference of the UMC in 1982 and has served many appointments in the Chicago area, including district superintendent for the Chicago Northwestern District. From 2006 to her retirement in 2024, she served the lead pastor for Euclid Avenue UMC in Oak Park, Illinois. Throughout her career, she has been an advocate for LGBTQ+ equality, ending racism, and combatting climate change.

Michelle Shrader

Rev. Michelle Shrader is pastor of Good Samaritan UMC in Tallahassee, Florida. Previously, she worked at Wells Memorial UMC in Jackson, Mississippi, served as lead pastor at Killian Pines UMC in Miami, Florida, as the Missions Initiative Specialist of the Southeast

District of the Florida Conference, and as Mission Enabler at Cape Hope District MCSA Office of the Bishop in South Africa.

Donna Simon

Rev. Donna Simon is pastor of St. Mark's Hope and Peace Lutheran Church in Kansas City, Missouri, where she has been since 2000. She works half time with the St. Mark's Church and half time as the Director of Evangelical Mission for the Central States Synod, where she shepherds congregations under formation and accompanies congregations undergoing renewal.

Donna Claycomb Sokol

Rev. Donna Claycomb Sokol is the pastor of Mount Vernon Place UMC in Washington, DC. From 2001 to 2005, she served as director of admissions for Duke Divinity School. Before being called to ministry, Sokol worked in DC, first as a White House intern in the Clinton administration and then on Capitol Hill as a staffer for Congressman Eric Fingerhut and Senator Tom Harkin.

Kristen Stoneking

Elected bishop in 2024, Kristen Stoneking is the episcopal leader of the Mountain Sky Conference in The United Methodist Church. Before her election to the episcopacy, Stoneking was associate professor of United Methodist Studies and Leadership at the Pacific School of Religion in Berkeley, California. Before this, she was Director of Ministry Innovation and Congregational Development and a District Superintendent in the California-Nevada Conference. From 2017 to

2023, she was pastor of Epworth United Methodist Church in Berkeley, and prior to that served as the national executive director of the Fellowship of Reconciliation. Earlier in her ministry, she was director and campus pastor of the Cal Aggie Christian Association and the Multifaith Living Community at UC Davis.

Marlon B. Tilghman

Rev. Marlon B. Tilghman is pastor of Ames UMC in Bel Air, Maryland. He has been a teacher and missionary to Zimbabwe, Africa, and has worked with labor unions across the United States. From 2016 to 2019 he was co-chair of BRIDGE Maryland Inc. and serves on the Executive Board of Gamaliel, Inc. He is also on the board of Project Transformation in Washington, DC, and Baltimore.

James D. Tindall Sr.

Bishop James D. Tindall Sr. is the Presiding Prelate of the Metropolitan Spiritual Churches of Christ. He resides in Kansas City, Missouri, and is the founder and president of the Urban Summit, a major Black advocacy group in the city. For many years he was the pastor of the Metropolitan Spiritual Church in Kansas City.

Jeremy Troxler

Rev. Jeremy Troxler is lead pastor of Guilford College UMC. Previously he served as pastor of Spruce Pine UMC in the mountains of western North Carolina, as the director of the Thriving Rural Communities Initiative at Duke Divinity School, as pastor of Maggie

Valley UMC, and as the President's Assistant serving on the island of Jersey within the Methodist Church of Great Britain.

Billy Vaughan

Rev. Billy Vaughan served on the faculty of the Memphis Theological School as Faculty Director of Formation for Ministry and co-director of the Center for Faith and Imagination. Prior to that he was dean/director of the Memphis School of Servant Leadership. His previous ministry settings include Patchwork Central in Evansville, Indiana, Plowshares Chapel House in rural west Tennessee, and Good Samaritan UMC in Memphis, Tennessee.

Deborah Weatherspoon

Rev. Deborah "Debbie" Weatherspoon is pastor of Epworth UMC in Berkeley, California. She is an experienced leader with nonprofit community boards and agencies and has a demonstrated history of working with multi-faith communities and in civic engagement. A strong community and social services professional, she holds a master's degree focused on Urban Ministry from Wesley Theological Seminary and is a graduate of the Doctor of Ministry in Public Engagement program.

Gary B. Williams

Rev. Gary B. Williams is pastor of Saint Mark LA UMC in the heart of South Los Angeles. An ordained elder in the California-Pacific Annual Conference, he is presently the co-chair of the CLUE Board of Directors. In the past, he has served on the General Board of Church and Society's 2019 Advisory Team, as chair of the Cal-Pac Conference Committee Working to End Mass Incarceration, and as chair of Strengthening the Black Church Conference Committee. He also founded Full Circle Recovery Ministry, a Christian based twelve-step group, and Faith in Action, a group working to end gun and gang violence in South LA.

Paul Witmer

Rev. Paul Witmer joined Women at the Well UMC, a United Methodist congregation located within the walls of the Iowa Correctional Institution in Mitchellville, Iowa, as a part-time minister of congregational care in 2016. Upon becoming full-time in 2017 took on the responsibility of coordinating the statewide reentry ministry. Previously, he was pastor of Covenant Christian Church (Disciples of Christ) in Urbandale, Iowa.

Janet Wolf

Rev. Janet Wolf is an ordained elder in The United Methodist Church and a professor at American Baptist College, an HBCU in Nashville, Tennessee. She has worked with Marian Wright Edelman and the Children's Defense Fund, the Children's Defense Fund's Freedom Schools, and the CDF Samuel DeWitt Proctor Institute and the Dale P. Andrews Freedom Seminary. She has pastored United Methodist churches in Nashville and served for twelve years as a community organizer around poverty rights. Her recent book, *Practicing*

Resurrection: The Gospel of Mark and Radical Discipleship was published by United Methodist Women in 2019. Her interview has been supplemented with material from that book.

Michael Zedek

Rabbi Michael Zedek has been a spiritual leader at Emanuel Congregation since 2004. Previously he was the chief executive officer of the Jewish Federation of Cincinnati (JFC). During his tenure, the Federation received national awards for innovative fundraising and programming. Prior to his service at the JFC, Rabbi Zedek was the senior rabbi of Temple B'nai Jehudah in Kansas City, Missouri, where he served for many years. A dedicated community activist, scholar, and teacher, Rabbi Zedek has received numerous awards, including a Fulbright-Hays Grant. He was also honored by the National Conference of Christian and Jews.

INTRODUCTION

I have noticed that the people who are good at justice ministry do a lot of small things very well. Years ago, as a student pastor working with the Ministerial Association in Haverhill, Massachusetts, I noticed that there were a couple of pastors who seemed simply to know how to do it. But, when I looked closer, most of their effectiveness seemed to come from what I now call *micro practices*—things like making phone calls, meeting key people for coffee, developing relationships with journalists, attending service clubs, cheerleading people in their own congregations, and supporting public leaders in key positions. They also sustained relationships with elected officials, such that they knew how to give appropriate praise in open meetings and appropriate criticism in private. (This is not the only way to address elected officials, but it worked in that setting.)

When I worked as the Director of Social Relations for the Massachusetts Council of Churches, I was the lobbyist for the council in the state legislature and administered its programs in civil rights, church and state, civil liberties, and international peace concerns. I became acquainted with any number of people who were quite effective in doing the work of justice ministry. One example was Luther McNair, an executive for the Massachusetts Civil Liberties Union. I was constantly amazed by how he kept an extraordinarily wide range of relationships with people in government, nonprofits, the church, Jewish defense agencies, secular organizations, and state and national legislatures.

I also noticed that he seldom was the center of attention or the one publicly directing the work around civil liberties. He made sure to take a position away from the spotlight even during events he had been heavily involved in preparing. He was an influential actor on Beacon Hill in civil liberties. My point is not that everyone in justice ministry should fashion themselves according to his model; approaches to justice work vary greatly as we shall see. Rather, I want to suggest that McNair used a wide range of micro practices that made him extraordinarily effective. He was a master of using face-to-face conversations to build relationships and connections bearing on civil liberties in Massachusetts. The way that he took people for a late afternoon serving of coffee and New England Black Bottom Pie was as masterful in its own way as Maria Callas's singing of Rossini's *"Una voce poco fa."*

In the civil rights movement, I found many small practices that often occurred in the backdrop and around the edges of big meetings, demonstrations, and other public efforts. I remember a wonderful story about the time Martin Luther King Jr. went to Greenwood, Mississippi, to support the organizing and voter registration program of the Student Non-Violent Coordination Committee (SNCC) there. One of the organizers, Endesha Ida Mae Holland, was alongside Dr. King as he led a community walk in a Black neighborhood, giving him the names of residents as they went past their houses. King asked

Holland about a woman they were approaching who was sitting on her porch. She told King that the woman was her mama, a mother of four children, and that she couldn't walk and was in a wheelchair because of dropsy. Holland said that her mother had once been a midwife and had provided rooms for "movement people." She added, "She like to eat sweets, she drink RC Cola, and she dip snuff." Holland did not tell King that her mother was resisting the voter registration project in Greenwood, largely out of her fear for her daughter and others.

When King got to Mrs. Holland's house, he went up on her porch, shook her hand, and asked how she was feeling. Her answer, "Toler'ble." King then asked a member of his traveling party, "Bernard, why don't you go to the store over there and get Mrs. Holland some ice cream, some RCs, and a jar of snuff?" With that, Mrs. Holland invited Dr. King to sit. As he made his way to a rocker on the porch, Mrs. Holland assured Dr. King that she would be registering to vote.[1]

I personally was engaged for thirty-two years in broad-based community organizing in Kansas City, Missouri, and in Phoenix, Arizona. If I needed any reminder of the value of micro practices, organizing provided it. It was my good pleasure to work with organizers like Michael Enriquez, Lora McDonald, Mike Miller, Jorge Montiel, Tara Raghuveer, Joe Rubio, Daniel Tucker, Paul Turner, Wilson Vance, and others. To apprentice to such masters is an extraordinary privilege. In this regard, I think of organizing as a skilled activity, one not learned only in getting things right in your head, but in developing honed practices working in a wide range of relationships, organizing efforts, and actions. It is a trained and participative knowing.

Several hundred of those practices are in the interviews here. Meanwhile, my academic reading and research gave me a theoretical backdrop against which I developed some conceptuality, learned to name some dynamics at work in them, and began to see certain macro connections.[2] More recently, I began to look for publications on micro practices in justice ministry. I found very little except in books on other subjects or in books on justice where these practices were not the focus. This is when I began to think of interviewing clergy who are effective in justice ministry across the United States. It seemed like the right thing to do.

What I discovered is that these clergy are *busy*. I called and emailed fifty-five pastors. I was successful in interviewing forty-three of them, the result of which you'll read in this text. The others, for whatever reason, did not respond to my messages. (I do not take that personally; my hunch is they were busy doing the work to which they are called.)

Please do not accuse me of personal boasting when I tell you how pleased I am with what I learned. There were times when I was profoundly informed; on other occasions I simply wept about the witness I found. There were even moments when I chilled with inspiration. I have never enjoyed writing a book as much as I have this one.

I do need to say a word about how I organized my learnings. I have not tried to systematize their responses. Instead, I have placed them roughly in chapters with certain themes. You will find that some topics occur in more than one chapter, as do interviewees themselves. I do not apologize for this, as the variety of their calls into ministry, the diversities of their contexts, the differences within their settings of ministry, the array of their skills, and the times in which they were operative all work against any thematic or conceptual rigidity.

My best hope is to get before you the comments of these clergy, whom I hold in such high regard, and through which, in listening to them and working with their stories, I found myself touched and deepened. I hope the same will be true with you.

I have tried to use their own language as much as possible, convinced that I did not want to move their commentary into my abstractions. When I make a summary comment or an observation growing from the interviews, I make sure that I have already reported the language and the concepts used by the clergy. I also sent to each clergy person a copy of my write-up of their interview so they could add to or correct my comments.

There are at least two ways to read this book. One is simply to read from page to page like any other book. The other way, however, is to use it as a devotional reading, using one selection a day for Advent or Lent or as a daily exercise during any time of the year. While I did not intentionally develop these selections as devotions, that's how I came to experience them as I wrote.

Equally important, you will not find criticism from me about what I learned from the justice ministries of these pastors. I see my job here not to critique but to curate, to gather and select micro practices from clergy who have the skills and craft to do justice. In this research I understood who my superiors were. I love the fact that *curate* means at least two things: as a noun, it means a "minister, pastor, or rector"; as a verb, it means "to select, organize, and look after the things in a collection, especially for a display or a publication."

Having a set of questions for the interviews makes it much easier to organize material, but a set of questions is also constraining. I sent long list of examples of micro practices in my formal letter to each clergy person, but I conducted open-ended interviews. I asked them to name *their* micro practices. At the end of the interview, I always asked, "Is there something you wish I had asked but didn't?" I asked several times, "Is there anything else?" Some of the resulting interviews did not have a lot of structure, so my job was to focus on the micro practices that were articulated.

It is also important to know that these interviews occurred from July 2022 to May 2023. With our publication date in 2025, some of the pastors have changed positions or retired. There also have been changes in the denominations and faith traditions some of them represent. I think here particularly of the change in my denomination The United Methodist Church, which went through a major split and removed from its rules all prohibitive language related to the leadership and pastoral care of persons who are LGBTQ+.

Even so, it is time to move into the interviews. To begin this discussion, I find it appropriate to begin with the topics of scripture and theology, as that's precisely where so many of the interviews begin.

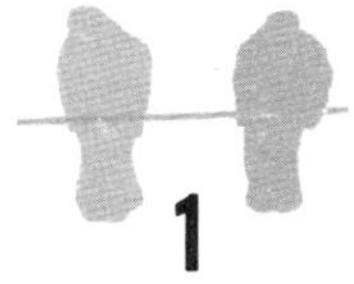

1

THE BIBLE

Drawing Justice and Community from the Biblical Text

Karen Anderson bases her ministry in the Bible. "I draw justice from the text," she says. She observes that "people tie scripture to what we do," and that "a basic function of scripture is to take us beyond the walls of our church." She contends, "If the community does not miss the church, then we have not done what we're here to do. The church does not exist just for the people inside." Her comments all occurred in our discussion of the centrality of scripture and its necessity as a guide to ministry.

In connection with her emphasis on scripture, she believes that people want to be whole and that the work of the church must address this. Food insecurity, for example, is always an issue, but "we teach and practice that God is a provider and that equity and the inclusion of all people are the work of the church." She then says, "In the feeding ministry of the church, we always pray. We are doing ministry, not charity work, and the grace of God is central to who we are and what we do."

But she is clear that they work in the community. They emphasize voter registration so that people have a voice, and they educate parishioners and the community on who is running for office so they can use their voices effectively. They hold community forums and discuss the roles of people like the governor and the attorney general so the people will be informed about what is at stake in health matters.

She points out that her city of Las Vegas is more than just the Strip. "There are communities here, and we must learn to adapt to new settings." For example, she tells me that there is a large Hispanic community in Las Vegas and that the church needs to be more intentional in relating to them. This means being available, but it also requires using Spanish in worship. Anderson finds that Hispanic people are going through many of the same struggles she encountered in her previous city, St. Louis, such as the rising cost of rent, problems in schools and with education, and many other things. "It just happens in a different language," she says.

Anderson emphasizes the necessity of truly watching what is going on and being observant. She looks for where she finds passion. She says, "People telegraph their feelings." She spoke of a woman who had been a leader in another situation, and Anderson helped her with a spiritual gifts assessment. She finds that it is life-altering when people find their gifts. This diagnosis/discovery is so important because "everyone has spiritual gifts; they just may not recognize them." Anderson firmly believes that God calls people into community, so it is important to look for the gifts that they bring to the church. Further, she maintains that people are called to the congregation, not to the pastor. Her job is to affirm and confirm people, to encourage them.

Basic to her work, as she understands it, is empowering people. This means giving them leeway. "I don't want to micromanage," she states. "If someone has an idea, I ask, 'When are you going to start?'" Then, she reports, "I'm there for them to encourage them." She makes it "a weekly practice in worship to thank people, those in the congregation, in the choir, on the board . . . everyone."

The more I worked my way back through this interview with Anderson, the more I appreciated her many subtle and small practices: being biblically centered; drawing justice from the text; working actively in the community on voter registration, education, and other issues; making sure that the feeding ministry included prayer; depending always on the grace of God; tying scripture to what they do; engaging in ministry beyond the walls of the church in Las Vegas; appreciating and working with the church as a community; being sensitive to the various communities found in Las Vegas, especially the Hispanic community; developing her powers of observation to recognize the passion of people and how they telegraph their feelings; providing spiritual gifts assessments of people and then making a place for them in the larger work of the church and community; encouraging, affirming, and confirming people; and refusing to micromanage but instead supporting the work of others.

I count at least seventeen practices that she performs skillfully. I came away from this interview convinced that such crucial practices play an important role in the ministries of justice. It is also clear that engaging with scripture is a *practiced* event. It is not only an act of reading—a micro practice in itself—but it is enacted, performed, a conveyance of the congregation beyond the walls of the church. Indeed, when the community does not miss the church, the church has failed to read and hear the text. As I listened to Anderson, I sensed a transubstantiation—scripture became justice.

Moved and Governed by Scripture

Traci Blackmon emphasized that "the *why* matters." She is centered in her faith and deeply committed to her "yes to God." She sees herself as "an apprentice to Jesus" with redemption as the goal. Even so, she is clear that there is both good *and* evil in all of us. And these are the reasons she shows up in the street for demonstrations. The goal of her ministry is not winning but rather reconciliation and discipleship, which she regards as "a mindset, a pastoral mindset."

In her acts of discipleship, she is moved and governed by "the truth of scripture." After working with other clergy in Ferguson, Missouri, and then dealing with the killing of Michael Brown by a police officer, she asserted in our interview, "The Bible is a collection of stories, and we are to be its keepers. Our job is to translate the truth of the stories in the street and to enter the pain there." In her view, to be in ministry is to engage in acts of discipleship, which is something that requires that we be "rooted theologically."

According to Blackmon, the most important thing is to be priestly/prophetic, not so much as an institution but as a gathering of people. In this work, she says, "It is so important to understand what God is asking of me. We are not out to beat someone—to win—but to be disciples. We are all created of God, recipients of God's grace, of God's mercy." She then asserted, "I actually believe the gospel. My action is discipleship. When people introduce me as an activist, I say I am a disciple of Jesus."

In the context of Ferguson and the murder of Michael Brown, I was jolted when Blackmon said, "Our enemies are not God's enemies." Then, in a reference to the Eucharist, she asked, "What if there is this table that none of us own, and we are all guests and hosts?" She observed that we are in a unique place right now where we don't have clear answers. We're having to deal with things that are antithetical to the gospel. "We use definitions to place ourselves in opposition to each other."

As I listened to her talk about belief, commitment, and conviction, I realized that one could take these in a subjective sense; that is, as if they are basically internal, psychologically inward expressions. But that would be to misread the words and fail to hear the actions in which these occurred. It was clear in our interview that these beliefs, commitments, and convictions were embodied. They were basic to an indwelling in the community; they were deeds of discipleship. Not only were they dispositions; they were micro practices.

Prisoner Pastor

James D. Tindall Sr., whose story we will discuss further in later chapters, was unjustly incarcerated for three years in Leavenworth Federal Penitentiary, where he became an informal chaplain to the inmates. His chaplaincy consisted of numerous small practices of listening, providing personal care, following up, being available, and showing up where inmates were. He spent time out in the yard, played catcher on the baseball team, and used those occasions to help the inmates with scripture and prayer to make it through the years of their incarceration.

Quite conversant with the criminal justice system and institutional racism, he reports listening to the inmates and then giving them scriptures. While praying with them he offered the Bible to get them in a state of mind to do the time. Maintaining that the right frame of mind in prison is spiritual, he advised inmates to get their minds together, assuring them that they could succeed while they were there. Once he gained permission to hold informal worship services among the inmates, he preached about Shadrach, Meshach, and Abednego (see Dan. 3). When he preaches about that story now, it's about his experience at Leavenworth: "And when I speak about Daniel being in the fiery furnace, I know who the fourth one was in the furnace. It was Christ."

I was interested in the way Tindall used scripture to interpret his own life in prison. He remembered the scripture when the people of Israel were given manna in the wilderness, or the way Elijah received nourishment. With humor, he reported a time when the guards—yes, *the guards*—at the prison brought him Gates BBQ. (Gates is a famous Kansas City establishment that many claim has the best barbecue in the world.)

But it went beyond food and nourishment. Tindall has diabetes. At Leavenworth he had to wear prison shoes and went to the doctor because his feet hurt, and the physician prescribed a pair of diabetic shoes to replace the standard penitentiary garb. When a new guard saw him without his prison shoes, he ordered Tindall to put them back on and took away the therapeutic ones. The next week, when his doctor returned to Leavenworth and found Tindall without his prescribed shoes, he called the warden, and within an hour the guards brought the appropriate pair to Tindall's cell, begging him to wear them.

I am simply amazed at how powerful micro practices became in the active ministry of Tindall in prison. Becoming the informal chaplain, showing up, playing on the baseball team, and just being there. But I noticed, too, his continual use of listening along with prayer and his work with scripture in placing the story of incarceration in the larger story of God's providential action—the God who provides manna in the wilderness and the Christ who shows up with Shadrach, Meshach, and Abednego. Moreover, he practiced daily, consistent encouragement to other inmates, giving them strength and the endurance to carry on and do their time in the right state of mind.

Hungering for Biblical Meat

And, of course, the Bible was used for study among the pastors we interviewed. Erin Counihan scheduled a Bible study on Wednesdays with older women who had been meeting together for a long time. "They loved Bible study," Counihan states. "We looked at Karoline Lewis' commentary on John.[3] One woman asked, 'Why did no one ever tell me this?'" Counihan reports that people are hungry for meaty academic stuff and are more than willing to ask the questions of what these stories tell us now. Unfortunately, churches often fail to offer these discussions and delve deep into the text, opting for pablum Bible studies when the people of the church are ready for serious engagement. Grappling with the text does not require high conceptual density or technical terms to be "meaty."

People Without a Pot to Pee In: Ministry in an Oral Culture

Sam Mann, a White man from Alabama, came from a decidedly oral culture. Yet he graduated from a fine college in Alabama—Birmingham Southern, where he was president of the student body—and from Duke Divinity School. At Duke he became a protégé of William H. Poteat, a scholar and theoretician. Poteat recognized Mann's grasp of complex ideas, how germane they were to discussions at hand, and their implications for action. Poteat also came to understand the oral culture out of which Mann thought and acted. Because of Poteat's sensibilities to Mann, he gave him his class examinations orally, at which he excelled.

Mann thinks in stories, relationships, proverbs, and quotations. The way he reads a book—and he reads a lot of books—drives me crazy. He will attach himself to one sentence or one phrase and continue to repeat and work on that phrase repeatedly, sometimes all day long! I have heard him find six or eight interpretations out of one phrase, and these readings seem ever and always to get back somehow to the poor and the dispossessed. The fish and the loaves, for example, are transformed into housing policy, good jobs, better schools, the organization of the poor, and liberation from the principalities and powers.

A conversation with Mann always requires tracing his comments through a shifting array of metaphors—biblical and theological, concrete and earthly, and always Jesus- and Spirit-filled. When I asked him about micro practices in his justice work, he referred to the line in the Lord's Prayer, "Give us this day our daily bread." He spoke of being nourished hourly and daily in his life. He then moved without transition into having faith like a mustard seed, part of his conviction about the importance of things small. Next, he shifted to the atom, something very small but powerful when split or fused. And after that to the feeding of the five thousand, where Jesus takes "two little McDonald hamburgers and feeds five thousand people."

But mainly he spoke of loaves and fishes and a crowd so hungry and so big that you take what you have and give it away—his point being that when this is done, there is enough. He illustrates this by remembering residents of public housing "who didn't have a pot to pee in" but who had hearts to respond to those who had even less.

To this point, Mann and his church built Parker Square, which offers 236 units of affordable housing. Toward the end of his ministry, they had developed four agencies working with the poor and the dispossessed. He concludes, "We had little people with big hearts. We did something with nothing." Then he had another thought: "Jesus is your introduction. He was born in a manger, but wise men came."

When I first got to know Mann, I thought he was incapable of discourse about social structures and systems; I have learned to keep listening. I have been in hundreds—yes, hundreds, some forty meetings a year for more than ten years—of meetings where he begins to talk, initially making no sense. But I have noticed time and again that people in the Black community listen and wait because they know he will get around to the point, and that the point will be relevant and trenchant.[4]

Mann describes his work as "living in the moment," and as is typical, he moves immediately to a story to embody the point. One

Sunday at Saint Mark's Church, a young woman came into the worship service. "She had been raped and beaten within an inch of her life the night before." She joined the procession at the beginning of the service. The members immediately saw her distress and stopped to help her. After that, someone who worked at a local agency for abused women took her to that agency to receive the help she required. Continuing his riff on loaves and fishes in our interview, Mann said, "You have to let the present feed you."

When I watch and listen to Mann, I become convinced that it is crucial to train clergy to communicate and function in an oral culture. We find these cultures in urban, small town, and rural America. This is true in many Black, Brown, and White cultures. I am aware that almost a third of our population is composed of college graduates, but it is also clear to me that there is still a larger plurality of people, not a majority perhaps, who engage the world orally rather than through some literary approach. Part of our problem in theological seminaries is that we train college graduates for an additional three years of graduate work to go out as honed literary practitioners to serve a great many churches that are far more oral in culture. No wonder we so often fail. If I had my way, one could not graduate from a theological school without significant training—not merely education—in ministry in an oral culture.[5]

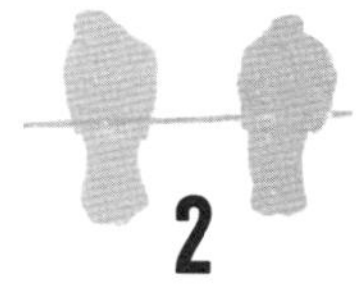

2

THEOLOGY

As you might expect, theology permeates these interviews. Time after time I found myself chilled, touched, moved, and enlivened by our conversations. Sometimes, I just broke out in laughter from the sheer enjoyment of how theology could come together with faithful reflections on the day-to-day events and small actions.

The Cradle Where Christ Is Laid

Donna Simon brought the Bible and theology together in an interesting way. She came out as a lesbian in seminary when the ELCA did not allow the ordination of openly gay and lesbian candidates. So, she joined Lutheran Lesbian and Gay Ministries, now known as Extraordinary Lutheran Ministries. She reports these organizations grew out of an exception that Martin Luther developed for accepting people for ordination outside the regular process when bishops were in error.

Simon referenced a metaphor that Luther used to argue against the inerrancy of scripture: "The Bible is the cradle wherein Christ is laid."[6]

Her use of Luther's distinction between Christ and the cradle spoke to something she had said in her response to my opening question about basic micro practices of justice. She said she just tries "to return to Jesus, to be in a close relationship with him." She offered that she sometimes gets "righteously indignant, and I need to control my anger. I try to put my feet where Jesus put his. I try to use his approach." Simon certainly honors the scriptures, and they play an important role in her thought and life. But when I asked for her basic practice in justice ministry, she did not go to a biblical text but went directly to her relationship with Jesus.

Having gone to seminary at Pacific Lutheran Seminary in San Francisco, Simon was trained in Christian nonviolence by Ken Butigan and Louis Vitale. She confessed that when she had been an undergraduate at San Francisco State University before seminary, they protested everything but didn't have "a whole lot of rationale." Butigan and Vitale changed that and helped her "understand the heart of Jesus." It made her recognize how deeply people need dignity and respect. She describes her time in San Francisco as "a life-altering experience."

"Especially crucial," she emphasized, "is learning that you have to be in relationship with people you are in ministry with and to recognize how utterly necessary it is for them to speak for themselves." Today, Simon is active with low-wage workers in Kansas City. She's been in their homes, worked with them in the community, gone on site with them at work, and joined with them in numerous protests.

I am touched by the centrality of Jesus to Simon's ministry and the crucial role of practices of relationship. A primary part of these relational practices is her own commitment to Christian nonviolence. This obviously relates to her presence in rallies and demonstrations, but I was intrigued that nonviolence shaped the character of a broad range of her social relationships. She speaks, of course, of how much people need dignity and respect, but notice her focus is on the homeless and the marginalized. It is crucial to her to be in relationship with the people with whom she is in ministry. Note also her clear sense that those on the margins must speak for themselves. So, she is active, day by day, week by week in solidarity with low-wage workers, organizing to increase the minimum wage, to develop human rights for the poor and the dispossessed, and to expand Medicaid. She can be found there in the streets, at City Hall, and in the state legislature to protest, all to be in a relationship with them. To her, this is to be in a close relationship with Jesus.

Theological Chops

In my interview with Erin Counihan, she was discussing social change, which we will come to later, and she offered, "You can change a lot if you have the 'theological chops' to make it work." She continued, "You have to know what is critical and what can be changed." Once she named this, I began looking for this kind of discernment in the other interviews.

Counihan used several illustrations of theological chops. For one thing, she worked hard on making worship uncomfortable. They tried singing in the round, which required that people listen to each other because they were singing paperless. They played musical chairs and asked people not to sit where they usually do. Counihan also led the service from the back of the room to change things up. She assured me that they always did these things in a faithful way. But she thinks that "being uncomfortable is especially important for White folks."

Having inherited a Christmas Eve service with songs and scripture, Counihan decided instead to use the church's people's own stories to reflect biblical narratives and provide contemporary events and illustrations. At one point they only used stories of women but didn't call attention to it. "People loved it." But the content changed as they moved along. She also indicated that she worked with the church and never changed things by herself. People loved the pace, the structure of the service. "They did not care about the texts; we could read anything." Then the people began to say, "We can change anything," opening the door to other innovations. Counihan points out that "the draw was the format; you could be flexible in that." She then quoted the well-known line from Ronald Heifetz, "What people resist is not change per se, but loss."

"Chops" is slang. I love the fact that in the Wiktionary, the first definition is "one's skill at musical interpretation and delivery; musical performance ability," which specifically stems from its origins in US jazz. A second definition not necessarily related to music is "skill at any endeavor; ability, talent, competency." Reflecting on this notion of chops names important issues for us in theology, in the work of ministry of any kind, and certainly in justice ministry. It is a performance that involves improvisation. It is clearly an interpretation that exposes us to mistakes and sour notes. But it is utterly necessary. Those of us who believe in the Incarnation, as I do, understand that God was in Christ as the Word "dwelt," "pitched tent," and "moved into the neighborhood" with us.[7]

As I listened to Counihan discuss theological chops, it became clear that she wanted always to be faithful. She worked to distinguish what is critical and important from what can be changed. She wants to break up any formal observance that had lost power and vitality, so she does this through discomfort. Part of her approach is to attempt new and current enactments, to use different stories, sing songs in the round, and lead the worship from the back of the room. But it is crucial to maintain the connection with people, so that improvisation maintains theological integrity. Further, she wants to make worship more communal by getting people to listen to each other in the very acts of liturgy. I see her practices as good examples of incarnate ministry.

I also thought of theological chops when I interviewed Stanley E. Basler about the effective prison ministry he had in Oklahoma for many years. Oklahoma is a culturally traditionalist state, and maintaining successful ministry in restorative justice there is no mean feat. One year he was working with the advocacy committee of the Oklahoma Conference of Churches. Being conversant with the state legislature, he said to an advocacy committee that they had no credibility because they were seen merely as "a bunch of liberal Democrats" by Oklahoma senators and representatives. Basler suggested that they break up into different advocacy groups and develop theological statements about why each specific issue of advocacy was important to people of faith. From then on, every time they sent a letter to a legislator they would attach a theological statement. It clarified where they stood and why.

I only want to say here that it seems to me of the utmost importance that the church not be the left wing of the Democratic Party or the right wing of the Republicans. This is why Basler's recommendation to the Oklahoma conference of churches is so important. My experience with lobbying and legislators is that very few of them are aware of the thoughtful theological and ethical stands growing out of Christian traditions—or any other traditions for that matter.

Bubble Up Theology

The term "bubble up theology" was coined by journalist John A. Lovelace in the *The United Methodist Reporter* in an article on the University UMC in Syracuse, New York, where Harold W. "Hal" Garman served as pastor. Lovelace characterizes it as the notion that the pastor and staff must "stay loose" and thereby free people up "to do things no one else could anticipate."[8]

In our interview, Garman says that he had "no grand designs" when he went to University Church—he just listened to everyone's ideas, and the ideas took off. Garman reminded me that Norman Vincent Peale had been a previous pastor there in the late nineteen twenties and had developed his idea of positive thinking in that congregation. By the time Garman became pastor, it was fifty years later, and the church was in decline, physically and spiritually. They thought they were dying. But then a member offered to raise money for needed building repairs and announced, "We can do it!" Soon everyone was saying it with enthusiasm.

The church discovered the energy to provide space for a neighborhood youth program run by Catholic Charities and to resettle one refugee family a year. They founded a pastoral counseling center to serve the entire county and began a day care center. The congregation also began working with the Urban League. Soon other projects started welling up from within the congregation. "My role was just to affirm their ideas," Garman says. "We did things in the neighborhood and in the city. We worked with Planned Parenthood, for example, when the Catholic bishop tried to close it down. I got my friends, and we pulled together pro-choice clergy. We would meet on the church steps at the same time the Catholic bishop held a protest. It forced the media to come to us as well."

In describing Garman's role as pastor, one layperson said, "Hal operates the blacksmith's bellows and heats up the sparks." In our interview, Garman said the process is "built on collaboration, really, a series of little stuff. It starts with little things—like a conversation between Jan [his spouse] and me. I then begin listening to the congregation, to the ideas for ministry bubbling up through them, not through committee meetings."

In another example, a pastor who had left Germany as a teenager retired to Syracuse. He and others in the congregation had been trying to develop a relationship with a church behind the Iron Curtain using the mail. One day he came to see Garman and wanted to make a phone call to the pastor of an East German church. This began a relationship between University Church and the one in East Germany. "We could build relationships, and we were open to new ideas," said Garman.

At one point, a group from the congregation built several houses in the neighborhood with Habitat for Humanity. After they reported back their observations, Garman preached a sermon about the need for more decent affordable housing in the neighborhood. A person new to the congregation came up following the service to volunteer his development experience; he quit his job so he could devote full-time to the housing issue.

People in the church became significantly involved in rehabilitating houses through a group that formed, Housing Visions Unlimited. Over the years this group developed projects in the smaller cities across upstate New York. "My role," says Garman, "is to affirm, to love, to be involved, and to get resources together."

The long and the short of it is that the congregation made a major turnaround during Garman's pastoral tenure. It became one of the most diverse congregations in the community with a strong reputation for its neighborhood programs and its outreach to Africa, the Middle East, and behind the Iron Curtain. They developed a full offering of Sunday school classes from toddlers to adult Bible studies; they held open issues forums and a special education adult class; their music program included a trained adult choir, a handbell ensemble, and a children's choir; and, of course, the church grew in worship, Sunday school attendance, the reception of new members, and baptisms.

Practicing Resurrection

To listen to Janet Wolf is to engage a swirl of actions, practices, spiritualities, theological reflections, and stories. I was inspired by her notion of "practicing resurrection"[9]—reading scripture where it takes on flesh. Practicing resurrection calls us to live in a beloved community, to participate in a kin-dom: "a new realm of relationship, radically egalitarian, dramatically diverse, shockingly inclusive, justice seeking, militant, but nonviolent beloved community."[10] In such settings, we find "visible glimpses of God's kin-dom among us." Practicing resurrection involves shifting from domination to collaboration and from hierarchical authoritarian positions to "doing theology from the bottom up." Practicing resurrection refuses to privilege "voices, stories, values, and decisions of the powerful, and instead to privilege "voices, stories, values, and decisions of those who are oppressed by structural violence."

Practicing resurrection involves a radical reorientation that places us in proximity with people who are poor, oppressed, marginalized, excluded, and silenced.

According to Wolf, "To be saved is not simply to be assured of some residence in heaven after we die, but to be liberated here and now from all the powers of death and domination, for abundant life and radical discipleship."[11] The discipleship of practicing resurrection requires that we unmask, identify, encounter, and take on "the forces of death, the systems and structures, the theologies and institutions of death-dealing powers and principalities." It is a communal mission committed to creating "a visible alternative to the domination system, a reflection of God's kin-dom."

So how does all of this get lived out in micro practices? Wolf lives out this militant nonviolent struggle with the dramatically diverse community that erupted at Hobson UMC, a community that holds her accountable and pushes her out of her privilege. It gets her into circles inside prisons, onto death row, and present at executions.

For Wolf, prison is church; it is there she sees people engaging in the practice of resurrection, a practice that defies the powers of death;

where communities of people love and live against the horrific odds of the captivities of our time.[12]

She sees the practice of resurrection in the way the National Council of Elders accompanies nonviolent movements. She sees resurrection in meeting with "a circle of women once a week where we can be ourselves, offering different visions of what needs to be done." Resurrection is mixing everything up by having potluck dinners surrounded by pictures of places and people different from those gathered, a constant reminder of the larger world.[13]

In the postscript of her book, *Practicing Resurrection*, Wolf states that her book has not prescribed the "right response." Rather, "The journey is ongoing for all of us. We are, day after day, liberated by the God of life, set free by the crucified and resurrected Nazarene, so that we might be partners with God in the ongoing work of liberation, freedom, and salvation in the world."[14]

Wolf has a story for every idea. In her postscript, she remembers a baptism at the Hobson church. One young man—living on the streets, battling with crack addiction and relentless depression and still dealing with old wounds of abuse and neglect—had attended the new member class. As he faced Wolf to receive the sacrament of welcome and initiation into the church, he turned toward the congregation with tears finding a way down his face and said quietly to Wolf, "I always thought you had to die to get to heaven. But here it is, all I've ever wanted: family that claims me, a place where I belong."[15]

As I listened to these pastors, I remembered that H. Richard Niebuhr said that God acts in all events, and it led me to think of all the micro occasions and all the ways these play into the providential work of God. I thought of the day-to-day moments where we live out the common hour that constitutes so much of our being in the world. The God who is active in all events would spend a great deal of time in the quotidian. I wonder too about the big stuff, the macro engagements and participations that we need to remember. But they are, in part, constituted of micro events and practices that are filled with lasting significance.

I confess that I am sometimes bored with the ordinary. It is hard to show up for committee meetings and be there when you would rather not; to make phone calls, to do the one-on-ones, to write letters and emails, and to listen when you don't have time to do one more thing; to touch base and express care for the person you really don't like, to deal with an asshole—all these things that Lena DeCicco, a social worker and good friend in Boston, called "scut work." And, yes, I understand that there really are some things not worth doing, but those are not the problem. The problem is that we often neglect important things that are not exciting or seem too small. I am convinced that God's providential work moves in these times and places. It strengthens me that the clergy involved in justice ministry confirm such an obvious but neglected reality.

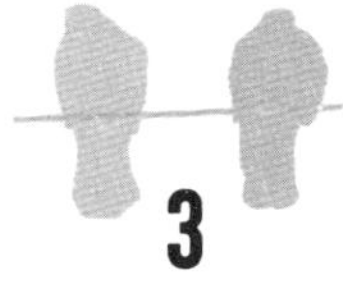

3
ON SPIRITUALITY

Spirituality is inseparable from scripture and theology. I distinguish it here only to throw spirituality into enough relief that it can expose the small practices of justice ministry.

Prayer as Posture, Scripture as Movement

Harriet Dennis said, "Without prayer, without divine connection, I could not make it. I can't do justice without conversation with God." After giving her life to Christ at thirteen, there's never been a time when she has not known Jesus, and there has never been a time when prayer was not alive in her life. For that reason, she asserts that "decency, love, and unmeasured impartiality are irreplaceable." She said, "Prayer is the posture, and scripture enables us to move. We are guided by scripture." She explained that prayer is necessary in justice work because it "helps to eat up the ego. It frees us to be wrong, chastised, to be intentional. It frees us from complete self-preservation, to build something for the lives of others. Moving into the presence of God has to be a regular practice of your life."

During the interview, Dennis reported that she had worked in church consulting for several years prior to the COVID pandemic. At one point, she asked God to "just let me ease back into justice ministry." She referenced Isaiah 59, a fierce critique of injustice and a forceful portrayal of God's justice. Dennis spoke of verse 15: "Truth is lacking, and whoever turns from evil is despoiled. The Lord saw it, and it displeased him that there was no justice." In response to this text, Dennis said, "God saw there was no justice, and God was offended. So, I said [to God], show me what offends you, and let it offend me." She acknowledged that she sometimes gets stuck in "the internal work, but that's where justice begins, in the internal."

One Breath at a Time

Bill Breeden, a Unitarian Universalist agnostic who is also "a little bit Christian," told me, "The only meditation I've been good at is taking one breath at a time. I only have this breath, and I want to give it back without hatred and animosity." He told the story of some teenagers who were driving in circles at maximum speeds in an intersection. A man got out of his car in a rage and got after them. In that moment, he died of a heart attack. Breeden does not want his life to end that way; he wants his "last breath to be one of loving attention, not anger and hate."

He continually tells himself, "The most important person in my life is the one in front of me at this very moment." He recalled being part of a protest at Indiana University where they ran into significant opposition. For Breeden, the overwhelming imperative was to engage the person who opposed him in a way that conveyed unconditional love. On another occasion, he preached a sermon on the economy in opposition to capitalism. People, of course, reacted. "I reminded myself in that circumstance that the best thing I could do was to remember my breath and that it must be given back in love."

He then recounted a Scott Peck story of a monastery where a Jewish hermit tells the three brothers who live there, "One of you may be the Messiah." That comment transformed their perception of each other, and people began to return to the monastery and live out its mission. Breeden commented, "I look for every person to teach me something. I am a student. The person in front of me may be the Messiah." He then summarized this part of the interview: "Justice is bigger than I am."

Network Spirituality

John Culp comes at spirituality differently. His mystical moments come when he pulls people together and gets them engaged in justice work. "I run ideas by people, test ideas on people. I'm a loner, but when I go to conferences, I'm the troublemaker." By this he means that he works continually to put people in touch, to network, to call people on the phone, and to go by their offices. "I am a volunteer chaplain. I go see people," he says.

Describing himself as a "compassionate, pastoral minister," he allows that he tells personal stories and identifies with pain. In his training in Clinical Pastoral Education, he learned, "I have to get to know my own crap to be able to help someone else with their crap. I love to help people. But I'm honest with them. I don't take an ice pick, though. I open them up gently, as a surgeon would."

Culp believes that God uses us, but being used by God requires that we "go into the wilderness." He emphasizes that we must be called, and that we must build friendships. This involves a range of practices like having lunches, communicating, and keeping up with people. He has "a spiritual call" to do these things. He can sense this vocation as a plan comes together. He has organized many groups around social issues by using invitations, giving people permission, and asking them to go on a mission. And after the trip, he continues to communicate with them. He believes that he gives "people permission to live."

He adds that one must have faith that it will happen. "You gotta do it," he says even though he realizes that this requires risk. He says straightforwardly, "I went to Africa and saw God." He understands that God is at a point where we have not yet arrived, but, he claims, he can "feel the vision," he can feel God leading him. For instance, he preached at a historical church where he attended in college and realized that the congregation was elderly and declining. Their vision was to save the beautiful church building. He talked to the president of the university, former ministers, church members, and people at the music school, asking the latter to purchase the property and use it as part of the school. "The vision came true; it was sacred and spiritual. These are mystical moments."

The Whole Identity Issue

Billy Vaughan discussed traditional practices like scripture study and sabbath keeping—more systematic approaches to spirituality than

Culp, Breeden, or Dennis. Emphasizing initially what he calls "the whole identity issue," he says the important question is not just how or what—but *who*—we are. He remembers a peace protest where people were shouting anger and hate. "That just did not seem to cut it for me," he said. This is an example of where, he suggests, both inward learning and outward learning must go together. "Our inward lives and our outward lives must match." He remembers spending time at the Church of the Savior in Washington, DC. While his churches engaged in very different ministries, he nevertheless went there and was shaped by the experience.

He realized out of that experience how much our practices ground us and what we are working for in terms of the church being an alternative community. For example, "Class meetings, the development of the small church within a larger church, getting a spiritual director, developing a small group to be accountable to, and so on," became extremely important. Of course, "some of these were disastrous," he says, meaning that some of these efforts did not work with specific groups. But he did find other groups where they engaged in daily prayer, serious engagement with scripture, journaling, keeping sabbath, and being in relationships with those on the margins of society. In these groups, he experienced the promise of transformation.

In other groups, they experienced real growth with the biblical text, "not just for preaching," he qualified, but "for walking with scripture." And for Vaughan, journaling on the texts became a lifelong passion and gift.

Quoting Jacques Ellul, he said, "Scripture asks us questions, but usually we are analyzing." We are busy making points, but "the Cain and Abel story, for example, asks us questions like 'Where is your brother?'" Here, journaling enables us to be engaged by the text and not use it only as an object of study. He pointed out that we can be so busy with the investigation and exploration of the biblical text that we ignore the questions a passage raises about us, our call, our identity, our mission, our context.

Vaughan then shifted to the matter of sabbath, where he gave credit to Walter Brueggemann. The sabbath, as he characterized it, "is not just a time to lay back, but a day to experience time differently." It's that interval where we learn not to take ourselves so seriously. "God's got this," he asserted, and he continued that, "We are participants in God's venture; we are not its determinants." Then, as his energy rose to the occasion, he claimed, "The sabbath is that time when we recognize that God is finally and ultimately sovereign." And, just to be clear, I heard no passivity from Vaughan in terms of the challenges of an unjust and violent world. Rather, I heard from him a time of sabbath when we see the world God has created and is creating, where we gather our bearings and ready ourselves to participate fully come Monday.

He then made it clear that our spirituality requires outward relationships with those outside the church. He especially means the poor, the oppressed, and the marginalized. In Vaughan's view, there is no substitute for these relationships. In this connection, he also spoke of the importance of being in prisons and of being with people who are inmates. These kinds of contacts and relationships with the incarcerated are central to his practices of spirituality.

A Formative, Transformative Peripatetic Vision of Spirituality

When Renae Extrum-Fernandez addressed the issue of spirituality, it was mainly outlining a vision informed by a rich history in the practices of formation and transformation. Having spent almost the entirety of her ministry in California around the Bay Area, she brings to her work the enormous challenges of her context. She has worked with Anglo, Tongan, and Black communities, as well as diverse Hispanic/Latino communities. Regarding her work with these ethnically mixed groups, she offered, "I want to build both the internal and the external spirit of the congregation."

She also stated that the growth of the church does not occur inside its walls but on the outside, beyond the congregation. At one time in her ministry, the small group movement had begun and was becoming widespread across the United States. It was in that context that she learned a lot about "the Wesleyan DNA for Christian formation." Once involved in this movement, she became acquainted with the ministry of Paul Cho in Korea. Cho used Wesley's method of discipleship groups to transform Korea to a country that is now 30 percent Christian.

She inserted at this point of the interview that those of us in the church in the United States "have lost sacrificial living. We have people who come to church who want to be fed. They don't care about other people. The crowd that comes, comes for the show. Nowadays, we are good at making members, but not making disciples." She continued, "We brought that on when we lost formation disciplines. We need to remember that John Wesley had to leave the congregation to make disciples beyond it."

She found that it was not enough to lead people to learn; they also had to be able to *discern*. The work of Eric Law, an Episcopal priest in Los Angeles, became a resource. He had developed spiritual practices for Christian community like mutual invitation and *lectio divina*. The former is a process "to ensure that everyone who wants to share has the opportunity to speak," while the latter is a monastic practice that makes use of scriptural reading, meditation, and prayer. Its work with scripture is not oriented around study of the text so much as an attempt to hear from the text the living word of God.[16] In one church that Extrum-Fernandez served, they organized seventy-two people in small groups discerning directions for a congregation that had been in decline for more than twenty years. "The purpose of these groups was to ask God, not each other, for the future direction of the congregation." Further, the discernment in these groups was corporate, not individual.

The spiritual work of these groups created "a community on the run. We don't need a club; we need a Wesleyan faith community. We need to get away from institutional expectations. Jesus and Wesley led movements, not congregations." She then shared two ideas with me. She introduced the first notion by stating, "Young people don't want to come to my church, but when we do a new mission, they swarm to it." For example, the church began working with citrus farms that have a gleaning program, which is the old idea of a farm leaving some of its produce in the field after harvest for people to come and pick what they need. They were able to get eighty people to collect citrus and take it to the Sacramento Food Bank. The next year they had a hundred people, and so it goes. She indicates that this growth "happens by word of mouth." It is "community on the fly."

At age sixty in 2018, Extrum-Fernandez and her husband, Paul, participated in the Camino de Santiago, a one-thousand-year-old pilgrimage in northern Spain. Seeing it as one form of "community on the fly, on the road," she told me that you walk five hundred miles across northern Spain. One reason she wanted to walk this pilgrimage was to find out what it means "to create Christian community peripatetically as Jesus did." She wanted "to find the kin-dom of God on the road." It was out of events like this that she took on the work of transformative ministry, meaning here that the church must take on the character of a movement and train people in the skills and the practices of such. Following Gil Rendle's distinction between managing and leading a congregation, she learned to be a trainer whose basic job was to show people that postmodernity has made much of what we do in pastoral ministry obsolete and that we must become a movement of Jesus again "on the way."[17]

Looking back over the interviews with Dennis, Breeden, Culp, Vaughan, and Extrum-Fernandez, I appreciate the diversity of ways in which spirituality is practiced. With Dennis, prayer is a posture—a necessary divine connection—and biblical reading enables movement, each of them utterly necessary in the work of justice. For Breeden, spirituality is centered in the practice of breathing one breath at a time. It is the act of breathing out love. It is a refusal of hate and a commitment to happiness for all as the highest virtue. With Culp, we find a network spirituality wherein pulling people together is the function of many actions, of identifying with pain, of putting people in touch, of moving into the wilderness of alienation, of being with those on the margins, and of a mysticism of visionary connections. Then with Vaughan, spirituality relates to the whole identity issue of who we are, the result, in part of an inward and outward leading, and the practices that ground us like "walking with scripture" and using sabbath to experience time differently. Finally, with Extrum-Fernandez, spiritual formation is vision, one filled and enriched by the practices of formation and transformation. It is the spirituality of a community on the move, a movement of Jesus, not an institution but a pilgrimage, a mission on the fly.

There are other authentic forms of spirituality than these, but there are more than enough directions identified by and suggested in the commitments made by these witnesses to the signal importance of acts and exercises of devotion in the pursuit of redemptive life and the work of justice.

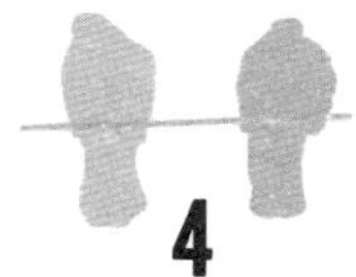

4
RELATIONSHIPS

Justice Work Begins Relationally

William H. Lamar IV said flatly, "Justice work begins relationally; you start by asking people their names." Who are they? Then, he asks them what makes them angry or joyful. "In Washington, DC, God intends for us to know people and to connect with their anger and joy." He recalls that for the last twenty years he has been fighting for true safety, not more police violence, and that he has been struggling finding housing for dislodged Black people. The powers-that-be have taken housing away from people, and "we have to do that with the same tools." That is, challenging the powers requires empowering those who struggle for safety, face police violations, and need affordable and adequate housing.

But he clarifies that it is not glamorous work. In DC, committed people must learn to live apart from celebrity culture and apart from American individualism. "We do all kinds of stuff with schools, with books, with pastoring." He emphasizes that these efforts must be "fueled by the Spirit." For Lamar, justice, politics, and spiritual work are one. Even in church administration, we must dwell in the Spirit, wrestle with the biblical text, and move into its resources. "For example," he says, "Jesus saw people; he actually saw people."

Lamar sees himself as working in the best of the Black and the prophetic traditions. He speaks with some frustration when he says that "the majority of the Black community is too accommodating to the larger society." This compliance with the world "flies in the face of Christ. Church is more than what we do on Sunday." In his own ethics, he attempts to perceive where God is acting in the community and in the world so he can join that work. "When workers get poverty wages, God opposes that. We need to catch up with God. We need to hear Mary in Luke where she says that God has filled the poor and sent the rich empty away."

Lamar continued, "We cannot be know-it-alls. We lead with questions, not with declarations. We need to hear the expressions of anger and beauty from others." He then referred to a comment by Ella Baker: "We must move the fog of empire away." That fog, he explained, is "the fog of war against human beings." He noted that "people think we [as clergy] are sanctimonious." For that reason, Lamar always uses his first name and never uses the title of "pastor" or "reverend."

I was interested especially in a comment Lamar made about working with government representatives. He said, "This is a small thing, but when we deal with elected officials, we take our reality to them. We begin with silence, with stillness; we just take a moment to come to be, and then move to the issue. We invoke the presence of the Spirit; we call on the Spirit." He went on to say that it's important to help legislators and bureaucrats see what they need to be and to bring people in need before them. In his experience, "politicians come to a meeting with a feeling, a sense, of what they will do, but our spiritual moment disrupts that." Public officials, he says, "need help seeing what they need to be. They need a view of love and justice among us all, for us all." He then added a comment about his own group in these negotiations. This procedure also places a claim on "who and what we are and what we take into those places with officials," suggesting that Lamar and his lobbying group must also be under the will and direction of the Spirit. "The spirit-soaked reality of Luke 4 is required. We are called to embody the new world, to embody that new world in time and space where the will of God is done."

Lamar then named a problem for Christians: "We are not trained to confront; we tend to comfort. We celebrate and congratulate, but we do not confront." He advised denominational bodies not to move people out of their professional positions who do God's work, but rather to protect prophetic people. He then summarized his work as follows: "The work of relationship is the work of the Spirit. I need to combine the best of the Black tradition and the prophetic tradition." He then added a word about joy that surprised me: "My ethic is to perceive where God is *enjoying* the work of the Spirit."

Lamar reminded me that joy is central to the work of the Spirit and the work of justice. I remembered how many times I have been so serious that I have failed to celebrate the joy of an action of the Spirit, of a moment when justice was truly done.

When I asked Lamar about self-care, he admitted that he doesn't do it as well as he should. But he did report that he exercises, listens to music, reads books, listens to podcasts, and loves to learn. He went on to say, "I am a rabid consumer of knowledge. I love to make connections." Regarding self-care, he spoke to the importance of family. His parents just celebrated fifty years of marriage, and Lamar said, "It is important to lift the young and to honor the old." He next spoke of the importance of ancestors, noting that Macon, Georgia, is his home. He told me that he communicates with his ancestors, drawing on the biblical claim that we are surrounded by a cloud of witnesses. He also used the metaphor of clothing, stating "I am clothed in my ancestors; we wear our ancestors." I heard this as a positive claim and thought immediately, of course, of the apostle Paul's suggestion that we put on the clothing of Christ (see Rom. 13:14 and Gal. 3:27). As sophisticated as Lamar is, he would know plenty about the ways in which at least some of his ancestors were socialized into their oppression and have worn the apparel of the principalities and powers, but I appreciated here the way he found a genealogy in the family witness of those who have gone before him. He suggested that it has been life giving.

Lamar dealt briefly with the problem of the resistance that he encounters in his justice work. He wisely suggested that he begins with his own, trying not to be "righteous." He invites the Spirit to dislodge him from his own intransigence to God's work and attempts to see his own refusals in the resistance of others. Even so, he believes "those under the Spirit can be moved." He understands that there are some things he cannot change, and, when he finds this, he attempts to work with others.

When I asked Lamar if there were anything he wished we had discussed, he said it is necessary to be present with people in moments of pain, when people are being killed, to be with church members, and with people in the community. "We must not be like Job's friends," he said. Listening is necessary; we must not use the time when another person is speaking to prepare our own comments for when they are done. It is not a time to look for a moment to speak. It is not a time to pass around clichés. It is a time to realize that we have no answers other than our presence.

After he made this point about listening, he raised one of the hardest questions we must ask. Lamar wondered if justice is possible in the United States. He noted, "Our foundation is so resistant." He wondered whether it could be repaired or must be demolished. He remembered that Richard Allen (founder and first bishop of the African Methodist Episcopal Church) had plans to resettle in Canada. He reminded me that Jeremiah Wright asked if it is possible to make a racist cake a good one. Lamar said, "I don't think we can change this cake." He stated that his voting rights were more protected under Reagan than now.

He contended that the church is one of the reasons we do not have democracy. "With congregations, it's hard to convince them to take on justice. [So as pastors] we balance the church as care for our members versus care for all, for justice." He states that, "In the United States you're either a White evangelical or a recovering White evangelical."

Here, I understood "White evangelicals" as having a concern for individual salvation and acts of mercy ministry, but not in engaging the systemic issues that hold people in captivity and require a response of justice. This means, as I understand him, that those who are recovering evangelicals have only begun to understand and act on the systemic domination and bondage of this country. Further, he observed, "We tend to keep Jesus out of Wall Street and the government, and we find a way for death-dealing theology." Consistent with this evaluation, later in the interview he said, "Polite culture hides brutality."

Then, almost immediately, Lamar moved to the matter of celebration and cheerleading. He named the importance of cheering people on, celebrating the good times, and honoring and commemorating every win. His realism noted the difficulty of getting people to knock on doors, that so many are afraid to speak out, and that these kinds of recalcitrant realities make it important to honor, mark, and observe everything that goes beyond them. Yet, he says, "We have to fight to keep on, to realize that this system is not permanent."

As I look back over Lamar's interview, I am struck by the juxtapositions. That justice work is relational. It is the combination of the best of the Black and prophetic traditions. One must take strong positions but realize that one does not know it all. That public officials are addressed first with silence and then with claims and demands. That we Christians are too eager to comfort but not to confront. That self-care involves family but is also clothed with ancestors. And, yes, we deal with resistance by first addressing our own. Further, to raise the question of the possibility of justice in the United States is to raise the problems posed by the church itself. And yet, we are called to celebrate every win. One may question how it is possible to keep such contrasts together, but if I were up against a wall of violation and oppression, I would want to be there with the leading of the Spirit and of Lamar.

Seeing and Being in the World Differently

According to Billy Vaughan, "Everything relates to relationships, to God, and to people." To do this connecting, we must know our narratives, and these narratives are both social and political; they are an interplay of personal and social stories.

While serving a multiracial church in Memphis, Vaughn met an elderly woman who regularly visited inmates in the nearby federal prison. She had an "astounding joy," and he knew he had to join her work. So he too began having one-on-one relational meetings with inmates. This, in turn, led him "even more deeply into issues of poverty, race, brokenness, money, and grace." Later, when he left as pastor of that church to work full time with the Servant Leadership School, some of the prisoners insisted he offer Servant Leadership classes in the prison. They wanted classes that took seriously their call to becoming and being Christian servant leaders. Unfortunately, after the attack on 9/11, another warden was assigned to the institution, one who wanted to be tough. "Because our classes offered space for prisoners to speak honestly about their lives, including their lives in prison, the warden decided that was subversive and placed listening devices in the rooms where we held our classes. And, finally, because I was protesting the war, they stopped the program and kicked me out."

But Vaughan was adamant about the importance of relationships to perception. "We need to listen relationally to other people's stories and to see the cultures of those stories. Slave labor operates in prison, and if you are not in relationship to these inmates you will not see the things that are happening." During this time, Vaughn and his family lived in a diverse neighborhood that helped them see the world in new ways. He used the example of working with people who were called "illegal aliens." He said, "I didn't like that language ten years ago, but with the ICE [U.S. Immigration and Customs Enforcement] raids that began to take place, it became not only offensive but actively destructive. We had to do something about it. We had to see and live in the world differently."

Relationships, Legality, and Systems

David Meredith emphasized the importance of peer relationships in working with immigration. Early in his ministry, he connected with a rabbi who was holding sessions with preschool children. He also cooperated with two pastors of a different denomination, one African American United Methodist and the other Disciples of Christ. They also had a sheriff working with them on this in North Cincinnati. This coalition between law enforcement and the diversity of denominational, interfaith, and interracial churches enabled them to help Cincinnati become a sanctuary city.

"Relationship leads to community," he says, "and we work with undocumented folks from Honduras, Guatemala, and the Congo primarily to influence public policy." He elaborates that for an immigrant family to work with them, that family must agree to be open about their undocumented status, and that means they must trust them. Another very important practice had to do with listening for the effects immigration had on immigrants and the existing community. For instance, they reached out to the nearby Otterbein retirement community for their perspectives, concerns, and help.

He spoke appreciatively of an attorney who was more conservative than he, but who provided invaluable legal assistance for the West Ohio Annual Conference of The United Methodist Church. This legal expertise enabled the conference to work within appropriate legal parameters while also enabling them to engage in actions that could challenge policies that were not legally proscribed. They learned how to be the kind of companion immigrant people needed and to address the legal issues that accompanied that kind of ministry.

Meredith had begun the relationship with the attorney simply with face-to-face practices like the table fellowship of meeting for a meal. They then began reading devotions on the Psalms, specifically on how to walk with people in their struggles. This biblical move also dealt with the church and its role in the immigrant undertaking.

Another significant step involved Meredith teaching others, which helped him understand all this better. The study, the work, the collaboration, the teaching: all of these opened avenues of action on immigration.

An interesting development from all of this occurred when the attorney became a pastor through a United Methodist program that trains and educates those who are interested in becoming licensed local pastors. This, in turn, led the attorney to become a pastor of an immigrant church. Today, Meredith and the attorney work online and with social media to connect with people across the country on the issue of immigration.

Meredith emphasizes how important it is to address the human reality within the larger system reality, to work with internal micro practices, and to deal with real people who are beloved. He is now quite glad to say that he and the attorney have become a unit, working together as a team on immigration.

Etiquette, Stupidity, Poetry, Outrage, and Beloved Community

Robert Lee Hill came to our interview prepared with several micro practices. Some were so small I would call them *micro* micro practices. He began with etiquette. Hill makes a point of always saying "thank you" and "good morning" and "good afternoon" to everyone.

But that was only half of his report here. He has a personal practice of praying "thank you" out loud when he is alone as a way of being grateful for being in God's presence. He says, "It is the expression of an effulgence of grace." Hill explains that he is trying to become a grateful human being because "half of what Jesus talked about were 'being' statements." So being grateful is important. This practice has become so much a part of him that he no longer consciously does it. "It just comes up." Quoting Romans 8, Hill believes that "the Spirit prays through us."

He also shared some practices that enable him to get through community meetings that he finds trying. Needing sometimes to respond to "something outlandishly dumb or existentially out-of-kilter," he has learned simply to tilt his head to one side. It gives him a way of responding without being inappropriately forthright. He has learned to scribble notes when he needs to "check out" and stop listening, an important practice for someone who participates so widely in organizations in the city.

He also keeps a journal, and most days, he reports, "I'll write something new I learned today." It may be a sentence or a paragraph or a longer piece. Also, in conversation, when he decides to share something of his thoughts or writing, "it is bite sized," and he loves having knowledge of the commonplace. In this context, Hill expressed appreciation for Kathleen Norris' *The Quotidian Mysteries*, which addresses the holiness of everyday work and the presence of God in liturgy, worship, and ordinary life.[18]

Sometimes, he enjoys saying something that has a barb, like suggesting outlawing groups like the Ku Klux Klan. In this regard, he noted how the Germans "did not outlaw Nazism in the Weimar Republic, but after World War II, you could not be a Nazi in the newly constituted Germany."

He also referenced translations of Dietrich Bonhoeffer's views on "stupidity." In the prologue to his letters and papers from prison, Bonhoeffer argued that stupidity is worse than evil because it can be so easily manipulated and used by evil. Bonhoeffer contended that stupidity accompanies the amassing of power; that is, when someone is in power, they abandon their critical capacities. Hill went on to highlight Bonhoeffer's thesis that nothing can be done with stupidity from the inside or by trying to change the perspective of a person caught up in stupidity. The challenge and eventual change must come from the outside, through liberation, which may include tragedy or cataclysm.

In these comments, I understand Hill to be warning about how vulnerable stupidity is to exploitation and how it requires an alternative, more compelling account of the situation. As Bonhoeffer emphasized, the change must come through some liberating act. I heard Hill saying that his use of small practices like barbs can be employed to confront and sometimes counter stupidity.

Hill believes that raising unusual notions is also an important strategy. It can interrupt a conversation headed the wrong way and disrupt a problematic consensus. But according to Hill, it also adds to the goodness of the world, "to the welling up, the overflow," and, again, "the effulgence of grace." Raising unusual notions is a strategy, but it is also part of the work of "beloved community." Being grateful, participating constructively and critically in the community, staying alert to the stupid, and doing the little things are of central importance.

You will not be surprised that Hill loves to tell stories. He drops quotes and poetry into conversations. He employs time-honored, personally validated aphorisms, especially when working with clergy colleagues and community organizations. He added that people consistently need two things: a sense of purpose and the experience of victory.

This led him to speak on the place of aphorisms, proverbs, and other words of wise practice in his marriage. He used the phrase "make the bed" as a shorthand reminder of all the practices of doing chores, tending a home, and making a marriage work. He said, "If I believe it all depends on me, maybe I will do my part."

Seven months after our interview, Hill called to tell me about a nightmare he had. In the dream, a friend of his, a now-deceased prominent Black clergyman in the city, had been denied the opportunity to play football for a certain college. In his sleep, Hill experienced torment and anger and awoke the next day still enraged, wondering where all that came from. The nightmare reminded Hill of the day he processed the profound impact of Martin Luther King Jr.'s assassination. He was at a summer camp in Texas and remembers slamming his hands on a table and shouting, "Why! Why!" and weeping uncontrollably. That response of pain and outrage, he told me, came from his parents, who taught him that all people are to be treated as children of God. He told me he had not had a good night's sleep since his nightmare, commenting, "I need to practice this anguish to be true to the best places I come from. I need to remain open to holiness, to a holy anguish about the deepest things we hold dear."

As I reflect on small routines of etiquette, gratitude, and civilities, I become aware of their significance. A telling statement, a fitting proverb or aphorism, or a poetic line confront and diffuse the lunacy and ignorance we encounter. Manners fit us for survival in meetings and personal relationships. These practices become the very embodiment of love and commitment. All these practices can form us for life together, even those that train us in the cultivation of holy outrage as an expression of beloved community.

To Be a Visitor in Someone's Life

Donna Claycomb Sokol says that to listen to someone's story is to be a visitor in their life and requires the proper etiquette. She attempts to "sit in someone's story as though in a home." She compared this to using a coaster while visiting someone's house; she says she would always use a coaster when offered something to drink. Similarly, she shows the courtesy of paying attention to someone's story to honor and respect the narrative. To use the coaster is to respect one's furniture, one's hospitality; it is to be a good guest. To listen to someone's story is to be a visitor in their lives, and profound courtesies are required.

But she took it a step further, asserting that we must allow stories to move and change us. She mentioned Jose Andre, the celebrated chef who won awards for both his cooking and his humanitarian work. He founded World Central Kitchen, a nonprofit devoted to providing meals in locations following natural disasters, for which Sokol says, "Andre gets down on the ground in crisis. He allows himself to be moved into action. He does not wait to have all things in place." Her point is that we need to get there, to act, and not to wait until all things are ready.

"We must allow ourselves to be disrupted, to show up at the scene of tragedy, to walk with, to write a letter, to connect with people." Sokol expanded her idea of being a visitor in other people's lives to emphasize the importance of going out as prophets.

Justice seekers need to realize their own abilities, that they have the capacity to influence others who are also called. Prophets are mentors, and sometimes it takes just one person saying yes to get others to come forward. She reported on a sermon she preached on Black Lives Matter that invited people to step up. At first, only one person responded. But then there were two, four, six, eight people who came forward and started a racial justice reading group. She said, "We don't have to have a big team. Just start with one." She was clear, too, that justice seekers need to be grounded in prayer and scripture. "Otherwise," she said, "we burn out, we fizzle out. We must have a *why* behind what we are doing."

She then described being on the receiving end of a prophetic witness. When she was the director of admissions at Duke Divinity School, they had an extraordinary entering student. The word was that he would be a bishop because of his personality, intelligence, and other gifts. After he had been at the school for a short time, however, he came to Sokol's office in tears. He divulged that he was gay and therefore could not serve in The United Methodist Church with its policies against the ordination of "practicing homosexuals." Hearing that story changed everything for her. "He was the same person he was on the day he applied. He was simply naming a core part of his identity." She reiterated that a story can make all the difference. It can alter your life. That's one reason she continues to listen and ask questions and then "do something different."

The encounter with the gay student raised the question of politics for her because "the capacity to produce effects on others is political." She says, "I do politics every time I preach." But the important thing is to get all of us in the church "arguing with Jesus." This last comment about "arguing with Jesus" struck me as theologically and strategically astute. Rather than articulating her own stand in certain circumstances, she has people directly engage Jesus's teaching on issues like citizenship and patriotism. If an argument follows, they are arguing with Jesus's teaching and not with her. Such engagements led her congregation to place citizenship in the kingdom of God before their citizenship as Americans. It led them to remove symbols of patriotism like the American flag from the sanctuary. They do not sing patriotic songs like "God Bless America," and they are very careful about how they pray. In the interview, I heard these comments as quite effective ways to deal with the idols of citizenship and patriotism. None of these things, of course, rules out an appropriate love of country and responsible citizenship.

I will never forget Sokol's comment that hearing a story is to be a visitor in someone's life and requires the appropriate etiquette. Such a sensibility comes from keeping your eyes and your heart open and from listening deeply. These are face-to-face foundational practices that require formation in the recesses of the things that tacitly hold us together and break loose in action. Because words, though necessary, are never enough, it should not be surprising that such sensibilities disrupt our ease and require our presence and our participation in locations of hurt and wrongdoing. When the direction of our lives and the pathways of our actions are not clear, it is time to argue with Jesus and remember which kingdom has our citizenship and our passport.

A Backyard Church, Narrative, and Pastoral Care

Cody Sanders describes the Old Cambridge Baptist Church as a very social-justice-oriented congregation dealing particularly with racial, ecological, and LGBTQ+ issues. He says his job is not to promote justice—the church is already doing that—but to tell the story to a larger audience. He used the efforts of the congregation's very effective actions around the 2016 national election. For example, they took on the violent rhetoric about women and queer people; they also stood with Muslims and the undocumented. They made the effort to communicate what they stood for and to say to these people, "You are not alone." During this time, many new people found the Old Cambridge Baptist Church. For example, one Muslim family came and joined the congregation as active members.

They put out signs on the church yard with messages about the church's concerns. After that, they placed a seven-foot cross on the lawn and attached metal tags to it indicating how many people had died from mass shootings that year. Their attendance went from about thirty-five to around eighty. He noted, "Almost every new person said something about the signs on the lawn, the cross, and about the kind of church we are."

They already had good, collegial relationships with other clergy, so they did not have to initiate these connections. Having been a sanctuary church in the eighties, they already had ties with six congregations that began to practice sanctuary with undocumented people again in 2016, which became a coalition of ten faith communities during this time. The relationships that already existed among the pastors made it possible to act more quickly and more effectively.

Sanders also mentioned that having colleagues committed to justice work kept him grounded and helped him with systemic and policy issues. Relationships like these keep him motivated so that he can then bring it down to the individual level. For instance, he told a story of working to get documentation for a family. Doing so, he worked with several other clergy and numerous laypeople, and while they did not change immigration policy, it changed the lives of that family. His congregants also worked together with people in prison. Two prisoners got degrees from Boston University, and one was paroled through the efforts of a circle of congregants.

Because they were a committed and active church, an important part of Sanders's ministry was to weave a narrative of social justice and to address the question of why these efforts are important. He claimed, "It's not just a smattering of acts, but a guiding narrative of our faith community." The challenge was how to get this said. Sanders maintains that giving attention to something pastorally validates it. He observed that people appreciate how important it is "when the pastor mentions something that people are doing on Sunday morning." He also underscored something we've heard any number of times before: The pastor must show up at events.

Coming from upstate South Carolina, Sanders always went to church. In fact, his father and grandfather built him a church in the backyard where he could preach and practice ministry when he was six years old. Originally a Southern Baptist, he came to recognize his same-sex attraction and then joined the Alliance of Baptists denomination. He shared with me about his partner, whose name is also Cody, and that they have been together six years. While his partner is not a member of Old Cambridge, he does actively support Sanders, which is very important in both his ministry and his life.

I was interested in how he handled justice ministry at a personal level. He divulged that he likes to take time to be alone to read and be outdoors. Making sure that Sunday morning relates to justice work is central to his personal and social life. And worship and music at the church provide "an intense communal experience." Describing one thing from the service, he finds the communal prayer which is opened by the singing bowls to be an aesthetic and spiritual high point.

Finally, he spoke of how pastoral care shapes his justice work. More specifically, his pastoral care courses "include the dimension of systemic issues like race, gender, and LGBTQ+." He understands, of course, that not everything is pathology in systemic issues—that is, systemic matters are not reducible to physical and mental illness only—but pathologies do offer serious cues to the harm of systemic wrong. He referenced one thing that he asks of students in his classes on pastoral care: They are to do something in their ministry contexts that affects people's lives in those communities. He reports that he is continually astounded by what students do, illustrating this with the story of a student working in hospice in a conservative area. The student put on a hospice workshop around the subject of LGBTQ+ people, which turned out to be a successful and effective piece of community work.

I lived in the Boston area for ten years, and I don't recall seeing signs and crosses in church yards communicating the social justice mission of local congregations. Working with other clergy; making a point of showing up; honoring his own gay identity and orientation; using his pastoral care training, competence, and sensibilities; nourished by worship and lifted up by singing bowls; doing these things in ways that combined pastoral care and social justice; and placing all these in a narrative of faith speak well of the training he received in a home-built church in his backyard while he was a little boy.

I See That, I See You

Ingrid McIntyre insists that you make work rich in fullness through the gifts of relationship—being present at births and deaths, being with people during marriages and baptisms. McIntyre understands that this seems so simple and yet is so important. It is especially crucial that people notice those who have been pushed to the margins, that they see them and then mark time with them through sacred moments. Sometimes this means putting markers on people's graves; other times it means speaking names in meetings or in worship. It involves sharing a story or deeply hearing one from another. Such acts acknowledge human value, presence in the world, our sacred worth, and the image of God in each one.

Further, it requires that we see the things that affect human lives that are different from our own. It is deeply important to be a witness to people's lives and everyday events, as well as to systemic wrongs that harm people for whom the system was intentionally not built. To say, "I see that," is a critical affirmation that these oppressive, marginalizing, and excluding powers are there and not just in one's imagination or the result of some fabrication. It is a way of saying, "You are not crazy; these things are real."

"The biggest thing," McIntyre says, "is to smile and say hello and to say, 'I see that, I see you.'" And, of course, McIntyre makes it clear that there is one thing more to say, "I am here. I am going to stand with you, if you want me to."

All of this "means putting yourself in spaces different from your norm." She points out, "It changes things up when you move into different places." She expressed her frustration with White people talking about race. "If you were really with someone whose life was on the line, you would have a different relationship," she says. She is clear, "We could be involved in radical change of dismantling systems of oppression if there were real relationship and proximity involved."

She admits that in her own accountability and discipleship, she needs people living within oppressive systems, people she can learn from, people who point to what's broken. Along with this, longevity of relationship is important, in part, because we need to know more of the story, we need to know more of what is urgent. "If I don't see the brokenness every day, if I'm not in the community with people struggling, I can't do it anymore." This also means being in places where she feels uncomfortable. It is a proximity with all people, with the LGBTQ+, the young, the old, those who are differently abled . . . EVERYONE—no exceptions. She needs presence and community.

And she says again, "We need each other's stories. We need each other."

Relational proximity is desperately important to move from empathy and aspiration to embodiment. It is not using your mouth only, but action, putting your body into it. It is an enactment, and it can be sacrificial. It is solidarity with people who are different. It means that we must question capitalism and the American dream. We need to live simply so that others can simply live. She also claims that if we were more in proximity, we would not be so divided. We are too busy attempting to create comfort instead of finding ourselves in shared experience.

We can also be interpreters of those who struggle, to make clear why the inequities we talk about (but others experience) are so important. She illustrated this comment with the story about a woman who gardens in the center of Nashville. Her ancestors were enslaved and now she owns three urban plots. For this woman, "to hold land is a transformative event. Surrounded by addiction, gun violence and poverty, people can be fed from her garden. People can thrive and not just survive." This is huge! McIntyre then interjects, "Small things change big things."

She emphasized, too, radical hospitality as "a big deal." Growing up as a preacher's kid, she felt like an outsider when they first went to a new church, but then they always experienced being welcomed by these congregations. She also grew up with grandparents who were always hospitable. Their conviction that "there's always room" shaped her thinking. So now, McIntyre wears a sweatshirt that says, "There's plenty of room at the table." This also means that there is always room for another perspective: "Obedience to God requires deep listening," she says (noting that she is still working on this point!).

She then commented about the need to be aware of resources so we can use them well and equitably. She argued for the organization of resources because these represent power. She says it's difficult to find people to invest in justice work, and for this reason, it's critical to be careful with assets and money. We also need to know our community, so we know where these resources are. We must not live and work in silos.

Today, people are wired by money, meaning that they are overextended with borrowing and debt. Too many people manage to get the best of everything for themselves, but that money needs to be used more equitably, she insists, because we have people living at risk of death every day. She concluded her statement about this issue by saying that she takes risks when she says things like this about resources, but that it needs to be said.

She next moved on to relationships with people of power. She told me about an encampment in Nashville and the need for affordable housing. She acknowledged that conversation needs to occur before action, and a group of allies in which she was active met with the mayor and the city and attended a park board meeting. The work was informative and reinforced her belief that conversation should take place before confrontation.

At this point, I asked what she wished I had asked her. She began by telling me how much it grieves her that justice work is not effective in the church. She states that our values are not reflected in our church budgets, and the talk of justice "freaks people out" in congregations. She grieves about the situation.

"One last thing," she said. "You have to bring people with you." Even when action groups go to the capitol to work for or against legislation, it's necessary to bring people who have never done it before. Representatives and senators need to hear all our voices. And we need to create pathways so that people can feel okay speaking up. She also spoke of going to the prison, to death watches right before executions. "It is our responsibility to bring people into those spaces of close proximity so that they can see what is going on, so they experience directly what is happening." She underscored the "intersectional character" of the prison population, the interlocked nature of class and race. "Poverty is a beast," she says, and the prison system is an unjust system that makes money off the backs of those living in poverty. This must be conveyed to the wider population, and there are no magic words by which it can be done. "There's no substitute for being present, *for being there*, for being in a relationship with others who are not just like me."

There is a great deal to reflect on in McIntyre's comments. Let me speak to just one matter that has stayed with me. It is the relationship between perception and proximity. According to McIntyre, proximity to injustice and pain radically forms perception. And I think she's right. It would also be true, certainly for her, that the relationships and experiences we have in proximal ties shape our capacities and readiness for action. For example, I know a half dozen people who have been present at executions. Their perceptions, their relationships with death row people, and their commitment to the end of the death penalty are lifelong, embodied convictions.

The point here—and McIntyre understands this very well—is that proximity alone does not make one, for example, opposed to the death penalty. It is worth learning the micro practices that constitute these differences, especially in relationship to the death penalty. I am not aware of a close study of the micro practices of those committed and those in opposition to the death penalty.

Nevertheless, there is a distance that refuses the work of the Spirit, that stifles the soul and disables the senses.

Contact, Brewology, Being Alive, and Anointing Things

My interview with Michelle Shrader brought a rich array of small practices around the issue of building relationships. She told me about making phone calls and attending a lot of meetings, about her interest in getting to know people, and about her efforts to make sure the channels of communication are clear for organizing. She disciplines herself to write seven letters a week to church or community leaders. Further, she plans to start what she calls "brewology," wherein an organized group gathers in a pub nearby for conversation. Actively working in ecumenical worship and interfaith settings, Shrader believes that "churches have become territorial," and she finds herself asking, "'What grows the kingdom of God?' rather than 'What grows my church?'" This question has pushed her into ecumenical and interfaith work that she sees leading to "a new creation" (see Rev. 21). She believes that this is a work of the Spirit—"It is an inspired thing."

As the interview went along, I was particularly interested in her practice of raising questions for building relationships. "It is important to ask good questions," she claims. In her conversations she asks, "What are the times we are in, and what is the best way to lead?"

These questions get us out of the "ain't it awful" complaint sessions that name problems but do not suggest directions or policy alternatives. In broad-based organizing, for example, we make a distinction between a social problem and an issue. A *social problem* is too big to deal with adequately. An *issue* is a matter that can be addressed. So, complaining about the environmental crisis is better countered with: "So what are we going to do about the toxic dumping that goes on in our town?"

Inevitably, too, Shrader also asks, "What makes you come alive?" Her ministry is directly concerned with the vitality of people. Indeed, questions like this open an entire range of issues, like the character of one's passions, the content of one's call, the aims or the goods of one's very life. This question of what makes you alive is crucial, theological, existential, and systemic. Pam Couture, who read and critiqued a section of the first draft this manuscript, reminds me that asking questions like this of people who are not usually addressed this way can show them respect and can be a form of compassion that takes on moral value of a unique, powerful, and potentially liberating kind.

Shrader also names house meetings in which she and several people assemble. She interjects that the meeting organizers are "task oriented," suggesting the complementarity of their gifts to her own in the work of such settings, and that Shrader needs other people. She recognizes that she cannot do everything and reported a time when she read, regarding boundaries, that a person is "not wired for some things. You don't have to fix everything." This taught her that she had to learn "to practice not saying yes to everything and encouraging others to do it."

Shrader has learned that micromanaging others does not give them the freedom they need to find their own way. Failing can sometimes be part of our learning process. She intentionally mentors or coaches her current leaders to know that part of leading others is not doing everything ourselves. There are different roles for everyone in the body of Christ, and she believes there is a way for every person to use their gifts to serve.

Shrader also told the story of a lay leader she works with at Good Samaritan Church. They have lunch most Fridays, and the lay leader attends meetings with Shrader. She also tags along to caucus meetings at the state capitol with other clergy, to gatherings in the larger community, to workshops, and so on. At one point, Shrader developed lymphoma, and the lay leader preached one of the Sundays in her absence. Over time, she heard her own call to ministry and is now becoming a Certified Lay Servant.

At the same time, Shrader makes a point of meeting regularly with people who hold her accountable to her commitments. My own suspicion is that, like the others interviewed here, Shrader does a great many things quite well. Still, she requires relationships that require answerability for her call and work.

Part of her accountability structure is the district superintendent, who is her conference supervisor in the United Methodist hierarchy. This district superintendent told her that she is "extremely talented at raising up leaders." I was not surprised. A good accountability structure not only names places for growth, but also identifies the capacities and the crafts of excellence one possesses.

Shrader says, "I anoint things." This means that she identifies, honors, and blesses people and settings that are important to the work of ministry and of justice. In my study of micro practices, I have become increasingly impressed by the role of ritual and have begun to acknowledge the importance of small, micro rituals. Their powers of celebration and commemoration are clear, but also their capacity for bonding, creating solidarity, shaping, and—I want to say—transforming people have a singular power. Shrader gets this and uses it effectively in her work. But as I write these words, my comment seems too instrumentalist. It sounds too means-oriented and not adequate to the way the Spirit operates in the sacramentals of church and community life. I remind myself that the Spirit moves in this world. The best of justice ministry participates in the invocation of the Spirit.

Craft

"Language is big," Gabrielle Kennedy comments to begin our interview. "How I name God is crucial." She elaborated that some people who work in justice don't work out of a faith context, so she uses language to try to open the door as wide as she can. She spoke appreciatively of her education at Eden Theological Seminary that taught her to talk about God and the Holy Spirit in ways that enable people to feel a part of the group and conversation. Sometimes, she doesn't use God as "he" but as "she," hoping to "identify a common ground with others so that all can find our way into each other's lives and thrive there." This gives other people the opportunity to use different language and avoid language that feels oppressive. She realizes that the church can be exclusive. Her use of language attempts to counter such things.

She works as well to discern what individuals and groups are going through, what's happening to them. It is necessary to understand context, and this is gained not only by reflection; it occurs by "doing stuff, being active, writing letters, and doing workshops. It is an active discernment." Kennedy says, "I do workshops, but an active discernment of the Spirit is part of those, not only do I ask, but I observe and engage. I feel the Spirit is active in those situations." So, she makes a point to observe and engage in practices that are spiritual. Her work as a congregational coordinator taught her to bring more people into conversations.

She gave an example of workshops on the effects of social structure and racism. Sometimes she is talking only to White audiences, but her message is about Black people. During one of these times, she was reading Martin Luther King Jr. in preparation for a workshop. Engaging with his message, it became clear to her that you must do this in a larger context. She said, "As a Black woman, I can just be angry all the time, so I need to find my voice on a spiritual basis, the little spiritual things. Spiritual practices and awareness are so important, and they are woven into my work."

As a pastor she preaches almost every week, but, she says, "Being a Christian is my primary job." She adds, "I do show up on Sunday, and I am the Black preacher in the preaching hour." So, in preparation for Sunday, she takes time to study, worship, pray, and write sermons. "I'm my own little worship story," she confides. She then clarifies, "Individual relationship is only a piece; it is not complete without community. The communal relation completes my relationship with the creation. God says, 'My people cry out to me; Let my people go.' So, it's not only what I do with myself but with fellowship, the church, and other groups. This is part of social justice." She underlines this point suggesting that we must not forget the God of the Exodus.

Kennedy is also a social justice organizer, which requires "the making of connections, finding common ground, finding commonality," she says. "We do things together, and those places where we find ourselves in community are so very important." Here she shared the importance of "feeling exercises" to get our bodies connected to our minds. We are often traumatized racially, personally, and socially, and we need practices that integrate our bodies with our feelings.

She then began to name exercises to activate and acknowledge our bodies and stressed the importance of breathing as well as the place of somatic practices in every meeting. "It's therapy," she said. "And everybody needs to have a therapy. In these exercises everyone is asked to talk about their condition and then to let go." They are instructed to pay attention to their shoulders, back, and hands and to focus on inequalities, oppression, and how these affect their bodies. "We know these," she explains, "by their impact on our bodies. We see these things in the community in dead bodies." Again, she corrects any tendency to see this as only an intellectual approach: "I talk to hundreds of people in all walks of life, and we feel with one another. If we see the problem coming out in the body, we must find a solution because, in part, it is *in* the body." She also does this with her husband, suggesting not only her confidence in these practices, but the role they play in her most personal relationship.

Next, Kennedy moved on to the partnering that community chaplains do with organizations and clinics. They have programs where they go and set up tents and provide services such as wound and chiropractic care. They have cooling tents and give out necessary items. Their clients include drug users and sex workers. The chaplain is there for them to have someone to talk to regardless of faith, status, or occupation. Kennedy finds that "unchurched people desire prayer and relationship." Recipients of the services come with multiple ailments, swollen forearms, joints that won't straighten out, and rotted teeth, among other wounds. The challenge, Kennedy asserts, is "to be able to take that in and to be present with them. To enable people to talk with you." She goes on to say, "Then we do somatic healing, a guided meditation, and a somatic spiritual approach with body and spirit."

Touched by the personal and communal character of her care and the intensity of some of these practices, I asked what keeps her at it. Her answer centered on understanding her original call: "I do what I do because it's what God created me for. Initially, I fought with God, but I ain't going back to the way I was before the call. I might need to change what I'm doing. I get quiet so I can see what God is doing." I did not hear this last comment so much as doubt about her practices as it was about remaining open to God's leading.

I pressed again about how she finds time to take care of herself. She said, "I don't interact; I take fewer phone calls. I take time with myself and God. I'm not out doing things, but being at home, chilling out, especially when I'm frustrated. Being still is important: Some things I have to do, but not a lot of extra things. I take one day at a time." She then shared, "A year and a half ago, things blew up. I withdrew just to hear what God wanted me to do." Then, after a moment, she said, "I'm accused of being a workaholic."

I also asked how she deals with problem people. Her answer was immediate: "I use a long-handled spoon. I deal with them, but I don't let them into my intimate space. Some things you just have to do, but not a lot of extra." She continued, "They may be annoying, but I pray about it. God helps me get over it. This ain't about me. God shows me how to work my way through this. They don't have to be my best friend. I have to love them. I don't have to like them." I remember being surprised when she named volunteer organizations as being the problem people. I would've thought that the clients were the ones who brought so many physical, emotional, social, and economic problems. She, however, didn't mention them.

After my interview with Kennedy, I was struck with how many practices there were at work in her justice ministry, and I am sure that I missed some. The practice of language and the naming of God to open the door for others to enter. Discernment as more than reflection only but as action. Spiritual practices, not as a sideline or private moment only, but woven into the work itself. Dealing with anger but seeing the larger picture. Meanwhile, finding her voice and seeing herself first as a Christian and then as a pastor. The desperate importance of being in a community; the work of social organizing and using feeling and somatic exercises. Her focus on the body and her role as a community chaplain dealing with the wounded. The centrality of her own call and the necessity of self-care while dealing with problem people in voluntary organizations. There is more, but I remember feeling that I was in the presence of craft—the refined, accomplished, skilled capaciousness of one versed in the know-how and the know-*why* of justice ministry.

Culture, the Homeless Home Association, and Scratching Backs

John Flowers began his interview with a relational emphasis on the culture of the church. This was central to everything he did when he pastored Travis Park UMC in San Antonio, Texas. He mentioned first the issue of those who came to the church asking for money.

Flowers admitted that it is natural to "want to cut them off because you've been through all the stories." But he asserts, "You have to hear the whole story even if you don't buy into it. Ninety-five percent of the stories did not surprise me, and 90 percent wanted to get money out of the church. But everybody deserves to tell their whole story."

Nevertheless, after listening, he asks questions. If someone reports that their mother is in the hospital, Flowers asks which hospital, indicating that he wants to send her flowers. These realistic, follow-up questions "often result in people stomping away." Flowers confessed that he often feels bad about not giving them money, but he stands firm, "We don't do money. We do food, we do medical clinics, we do recovery groups." In fact, he said, "I would overwhelm people who had requests with all that we were doing." But he emphasized that he would listen, he would be present, and he would not cut them off.

I was struck, too, by the way the congregation set up their health clinic on a relational basis. Flowers tells the story of a county agency that came to talk with him on a Sunday morning. They wanted to set up the church with clinics and other services. Flowers did not make that decision but invited the county people downstairs to talk with those served by the church. The county agency people asked the homeless why they went to Travis Park UMC. Their answer was, "Because they know my name," and that "with the county, I'm just a number."

The county people wanted to bring their clinic to the church, but Flowers said, "This is not a medical clinic that has a church, but a church that has a clinic." They were willing for the clinic to come, but "they had to do it with our approach." Flowers explained, "This is not a medical delivery model; this is a wholeness, wellness model." He elaborated that the county had to learn from the people they served; they had to learn their names and who they are. Further, Flowers emphasized that there had to be equity of power between the people and the county clinic. He specified that doctors are not to behave as if the people are merely recipients of services. The county people said no. But Flowers held firm. He was convinced that dignity and respect depend on equity of power, and that the homeless must have power in a relationship with any clinic that would work from the church. So, the church got doctors and other staff through its own resources, people who would work with a wholeness, wellness model.

Flowers reported another example. The homeless people of the church came from the general neighborhood around it. At night people were sleeping around the building. So, Flowers "got together the most functional homeless people," and they became "the homeowners association." They established rules: "The number one rule was that you have to clean up your site and be out of there by seven o'clock in the morning. You have to keep it clean and be gone." This rule was needed, says Flowers, "to make sure they didn't stay too long and therefore make it harder for us to do the work."

But there were other practices Flowers enacted. He made a point to eat regularly with homeless people at church. He "teased and played" with them. "You got to play with them," he emphasized. "You've got to scratch their backs." It was this kind of ongoing, high contact, personal relationship with the people around the church that contributed greatly to the effectiveness of Flowers and the work of Travis Park UMC.

Partnerships, Engaging People

Gary B. Williams began our interview by telling me that he is a recovering addict who has been convicted of crimes, and this is the lens through which he sees the world. When we met in September 2022, he had been clean and sober for nineteen years and eight months. Because of this background, he "feels connected to those on the margins and to undocumented sisters and brothers."

He is co-chair of Clergy/Laity United for Economic Justice (CLUE). Founded by James Lawson, CLUE brings together clergy and lay leaders of all faiths with the marginalized, the unheard, and the least protected in the cause of a just economy that works for everyone, not just those at the top. They support union workers for fair wages.

Williams tells me that in 2015 he was pastoring two churches, one in a gang-controlled neighborhood. When a young man was killed across the street from his church and another young man murdered in the area, the people of Faith UMC said, "That's enough." Williams and others in the community determined that they were going to do something about it. They connected with LA Voice, and together they initiated a local chapter of Faith in Action, which is "a national community organizing network that gives people of faith the tools that they need to fight for justice and work towards a more equitable society."[19]

With this, the community around them began to understand that they were involved. Williams reports, "This was my first time to do a funeral for a gang member; four hundred people were there." During the funeral, Williams asked three questions of those gathered: "Don't you want better for your own children? Which one of you will step up and be a father to the dead man's children? Which of you will get involved in intervention to resolve issues without violence?" After that, they began meeting weekly in gang interventions.

With the coming of the pandemic, the church got further involved with the issue of food inequality. They had been giving out food once a month, but now people were coming every week. So, Williams and his wife found new ways to get food. The church was in a food desert he describes as, "really a food apartheid within a five-mile radius." They became connected with a food scientist who was a member of the AME Church. They began a labyrinthine food garden and were able to give away all the food they grew. Further, they were working on twenty-one units of affordable housing on a 9,500 square-foot property adjacent to the church, turning it into a farm with a community gathering space and a new church place based on food justice.

They then developed a partnership with Kounkuey Design Initiative (KDI), a community development and design nonprofit that "partners with under-resourced communities to advance equity and activate unrealized potential in their neighborhoods and cities."[20] Williams elaborates that KDI helps the community find funding. Moreover, in that part of Los Angeles, where there are no food markets, they also work with Bread for the World, which has an organizer there. They also lobby in Washington, DC, and receive training and help with elected officials.

I asked how he makes these things happen in a local church like Saint Mark. He said he works through a core group of people and sprinkles things in messages to the congregation and to individuals. He finds, "The people do what I do." He informed me that his family lives in the parsonage next to the church and are the first pastoral family to do that in some time. People also know who he is when he walks the street, and sometimes he invites organizers to come into the church and speak in worship and in meetings. They also do voter registration and get other people to talk about issues. They go to the city council, and they have a neighborhood council in the area.

He added, "Being a recovering addict myself, we support Narcotics Anonymous meetings. This opens the door for new members because they know who I am." Further, "We stay connected with the community. We are the church in the heart of the community and with the community in our heart. We are intentional." They have Fentanyl awareness day and invite the school of pharmacy at the University of Southern California to come in to help. They work with the LGBTQ+ community and with other young adults. These connections are crucial, he says, because "networking, getting to know people, builds community and relates the church to wider circles of people."

Another important partner is the Homeless Outreach Program Integrated Care System (HOPICS), which is the leading homeless service agency in the Service Planning Area 6, servicing South Los Angeles, Paramount, Compton, & Lynwood.[21] "It is a homeless outreach service," Williams explains, "and two of our church members work for them. We are encouraging Black churches to get involved in projects, for example, working with young people who get kicked out of the house." Williams sat in and worked with the facilitation process and told the facilitator he wanted Saint Mark to be a part of the work. "We were the only church to sign up. We got $5,000 for a room for families to meet so we can rejuvenate our workspace."

In their work with guns and gang violence, they received a $180,000 grant to disperse AIDS tests that people can pick up at the church or receive by mail. Further, they hired a young person to update their website.

I asked Williams for more specific micro practices they use. He told me he invites workers in the church to share ideas in one-on-ones. He also gets people involved and encourages them to take on leadership roles. Saint Mark also has a young woman on the deacon track in the United Methodist ordination system, and she takes on some of the work. "We bring people along, get a sense of where they are, and then get them involved." He is always on the lookout for the right people for the right tasks.

Another thing he does is make use of an automated call system. Four times a week, he records a two-minute reflection that includes a short prayer and scripture. He also sends it out to the homeless who have access to phones, and they now have three hundred people after two years who engage with it.

He concluded these comments about micro practices by saying, "The most important small thing is to continue to engage people." He reminds himself that he is not in this alone. He says, "You have to shine your light and be ready to talk about what you're doing all the time. You must continually create new partnerships."

Impressed with Williams's Herculean effort, or should I say grace-filled energy, I asked how he takes care of himself. He shares that he has a spiritual guide, a mentor. She is co-chair of CLUE and a Buddhist, and she instructs him on meditation. But he confesses, "It comes along slow." He also admits that self-care did not come easily for him. "I didn't do well at first." But now he works out with other people, exercising forty-five minutes a day, Monday through Friday. His family takes time off for vacation, and he regularly travels to Iowa to see a former member and take a break. He also found respite by taking a trip to Alabama as a breather from the daily work. He also takes breaks from the daily work by participating in rallies and demonstrations around the country.

Among the clergy I interviewed, networking, relationship building, and pulling together agencies and organizations were important practices, but no one did more with this than Williams. Living in the neighborhood and making himself known on the street; developing ties with CLUE as well as with workers, gangs, and food resource people; developing affordable housing; partnering with KDI, Bread for the World, and the USC School of Pharmacy; reaching out to the homeless; organizing with workers; finding talented persons; getting people involved and encouraging leadership; delegating tasks to others; the use of automated calling; and the central impulse of engaging people. Williams models this form of urban ministry in a complex metropolitan area. Partnerships formed initially with a plethora of micro practices are a key component of justice ministry today.

5

DOING CHANGE, PART 1

I suspect that the hardest problem one has when interviewing highly competent people is that they know a great deal more than they can say. Their tacit knowledge exceeds their explicit articulation. Further, some of the best comments come in asides to another matter. Not only for this chapter, but especially for this chapter, I have gone back and forth over the interviews many times to make sure I haven't missed references to what it means to do social change. I forewarn you of this as a reader, because I want you to listen for the assumptions behind their stated claims.

Neighborhood Exegesis

I begin this section on doing change with a concept used by Erin Counihan: "neighborhood exegesis." Her first pastorate was in St. Louis, and she became deeply involved in the issue of the police killing of Michael Brown in Ferguson, Missouri, a suburb of that larger city.

Her congregation, Oak Hill Presbyterian Church, was already involved in community organizing as part of a Gamaliel project, and Counihan reports that she "leaned into" the protest of Brown's homicide.

Crucial to her work at the beginning of her pastorate was neighborhood exegesis. She asked questions, such as "What's here? What's not here? Who is here doing things in the daytime? Who's doing them in the evening?"[22]

Using community organizing principles such as one-on-one relational meetings, Counihan got to know neighborhood people. She also went on neighborhood walks, knocking on doors and talking with people. As a result of the knowledge she gained from her neighborhood exegesis, her church began several new programs and practices.

The church started a new series, "Issues among Us," in which they went to museum exhibits, notably one on gun violence, and then talked about what they had seen. They made sure they had something for kids on the days school was out. They started with Martin Luther King Jr. Day and found that they had a lot of children from the neighborhood but not from the church. So, the next year, they also did a Martin Luther King Jr. worship service. After Ferguson, they decided to make the MLK Day commemoration about learning. They took rides up to the cemetery to study important African Americans in the city. They also went to the jail to talk about cash bail, mass incarceration, and racism. They would then go to lunch to talk about what they had seen, and they would ask kids to write letters to the mayor and coach them on how to do that.

The city has no walk-up shelters, so Oak Hill Church provided a shelter once a week and used that occasion to write letters to officials. They met with neighborhood representatives and aldermen, with whom they would often engage outside. They were also interested in Jefferson City—the state capital in Missouri—and invited state representatives and senators to come talk with them. One state senator came but kept his remarks much too vague, so church people asked him, "How do we get anything done statewide?" Counihan states that at that point he did help with instruction. Further, they organized an Artivist House, combining the word "artist" and "activist." This work taught art through activism and activism through art, using art to express action and action to initiate art.

As I listened to Counihan, I realized that all the things I just reported are forms of neighborhood exegesis in her ministry. I was struck that this kind of analysis is not only a desk-based activity—certainly not taking place in an ivory tower—but an engaged, relational, out-in-the-community, people-involved, action form of exegesis. Clearly, a great deal of reflection must have occurred prior to and in the execution of this embodied, social, and conduct-oriented form of "reading" the community. Neighborhood exegesis in Counihan's terms is the work in and of a community, which is a significant contribution of the micro practices of justice ministry.

Being There and Pitching Tent

Renae Extrum-Fernandez had her first pastoral appointment in San Francisco during the AIDS epidemic. She was in a Spanish-speaking congregation of about fifty members, virtually all of them political and economic refugees, and every one of them impacted in some way by AIDS. Fearful of contagion and the stigma of homosexuality, clergy connected with people in the Latino community would not visit AIDS patients. Extrum-Fernandez was fearful of doing so herself, as she was pregnant, and little was known about the transmission of HIV. But she had heard about medieval clergy who visited sick people during the plagues, and so she went.

One of her early visits was with a little boy with Down syndrome who had been given blood that contained the AIDS virus when he had heart surgery. During her visit with him, his mother asked, "Why would God give AIDS to a Down syndrome, undocumented child with heart issues?" This was a powerful moment that has continued to form her throughout her ministry. Working with that mother and her child set the mandate in place for "being there" in ministry.

In this first appointment in San Francisco, there were seven nations represented in her church and community, and they helped her learn the complexity of Spanish as she worked in liturgy and other settings. Her own Spanish was "imbued with the Aztec language, so it was tricky to include everyone because you want to use the idioms of each dialect." While she had experienced some diversity among Latino people as a seminary student, she was dropped into a ministerial situation that was far more diverse and was given little to no training. Even so, they started a community center, got grants, and, thankfully, hired a young woman from El Salvador who was acculturated to the United States, spoke English very well, and was familiar with the city. They also connected with immigration lawyers who helped people get settled in the community and deal with the range of legal issues regarding undocumented people.

Her next appointment took her to Palo Alto where she served as an associate pastor. It was quite a shift, and she liked working on a team. Palo Alto is an affluent, privileged community, but East Palo

Alto is where poor people of all races and nations live. It was an eye-opening experience for her to discover how insulated affluent Palo Alto is. She found there was an invisible wall, and that the real issue was not racial or interethnic but interclass.

Her ministry there involved Tongan people. She learned the Tongan language and found similarities between their poverty and immigration issues and those in her first church. She followed United Methodist polity by beginning with this group as a fellowship and then having them become members of the church.

From there she went to Walnut Creek UMC near Oakland, which felt more like the diverse community she, a Latino Protestant raised in a Roman Catholic town, had been born into. She was home! There, too, the diversity of the wider community was part of her church. There were Euro-Americans, African Americans, Filipinos, and extended Mexican families, though the church itself was not diverse, and she was the first woman to be the lead pastor.

I loved her story about how she started a community-outreach ministry when she was first at Walnut Creek. There was an alleyway between the church and an apartment building. One day she heard noises outside her office window. Parting the curtains she saw flames in the alley and called the fire department. When Extrum-Fernandez ran to the spot, she saw a group of little boys who had piled up paper and books and set them on fire! Seeing her, they scattered like scared mice—all but one, who was stuck in the middle of their bicycles. She said, "We're going to put out that fire and then we are going to put all those bikes in my office and call your parents." She told people in the church, "When God sends you a burning bush, you need to act." And so, inspired by those kids, they set up an after-school tutoring program that still exists today.

I am struck by the diverse contexts of the ministry of Extrum-Fernandez, by the demands required by the range of peoples to whom she ministered. She spoke of the cultural skills that are required, but she knows and does much more than she had time to name in our interview. This means that "being there" requires a presence, and by no means do I want to suggest any diminution of its importance. At the same time, "being there" requires not only closeness, but the skilled capacities, the cultural moves—the honed micro practices—to be there *fully*. The necessity of knowing the language, the sensitivity to the struggle and the tragedy of people's lives in their context—the meaning of looks or gestures; of popular wisdom; of music and art; of the subtleties of acceptance, embarrassment, and "kinship;" or of what can be said and heard spiritually—these are among the practices, indeed, that suggest the holistic grasp of a situation or a meeting, or a pastoral moment, or the voicing of claims in sermons and teaching and baptisms and funerals. Think, then, of all these and more in doing justice ministry.

I read Gustavo Gutierrez's *A Theology of Liberation* back in the mid-seventies, and it changed my understanding of the Incarnation. He spoke about that famous passage in John 1:14 that says, "So the word became flesh; he came to dwell [pitch his tent] among us."[23] Gutierrez argued that Christ pitches his tent (the Greek word is *skennoo*) with us, that Christ presents himself as the temple of God (John 4:21-23), and that he has joined the world in that act of indwelling, of disclosure and action in the world.

These few passages in Gutierrez led me to considerable contemplation about what it means when God pitched tent with us in Christ. By that very act, God joins the local practices of a culture of dwelling with us. I thought of Christ as a human being living in Nazareth; growing up with Mary and Joseph; speaking in the local idiom of Aramaic; using the practices of storytelling and proverbs; teaching about birds, sheep, sewers, and house builders; identifying with the poor and the dispossessed; being formed as a Jew by the ancient texts of Judaism; recruiting his disciples from among the peasants; and traveling the land by foot. In being human, Christ was thoroughly local, a claim that in no way takes away from his being divine. The Incarnation included being there and being profoundly local, not parochial, but divinely local.

Ever since reading Gutierrez, I have worked at developing ministry in its various forms in terms of this understanding of the Incarnation. It is no advocacy of accommodation to the principalities and powers. Paul speaks to us in Romans 12:2, "Do not be conformed to this world, but be transformed by the renewing of your minds, so that you may discern what is the will of God—what is good and acceptable and perfect" (NRSVA).

Further, in suggesting a local form of ministry, I absolutely do not mean that the European American understanding/approach is the real, cosmopolitan one, and that the faith of others is a local expression. All our expressions of faith are local—perhaps none more so than the highly literate, privileged, affluent, cultural context I represent.

I question the label "cosmopolitan" as applied to anyone. One exception might be a seller of local goods in a place like Nairobi where he or she has had to learn six or seven languages and negotiate with a wide range of persons who come to that town from across the world. I remember a story told by Clifford Geertz about an anthropologist who had characterized a local tradesman in a crossroads village as local and non-cosmopolitan. Geertz observed that that local tradesman had probably engaged more people from across the world than the scholarly, academic anthropologist ever would.

Another example, I served thirty-two years as a professor at Saint Paul School of Theology and have since been on its board and also on the advisory board of another seminary. I know presidents, deans, and faculty across the United States. Sometimes one of them will speak of having a "global point of view," which I find ludicrous. I have never met anyone who has a global point of view, including myself of course.

I do not mean we should ignore people of other cultures in the world. It is crucial that we respect the mystery of people who are other. If we do not, if we mindlessly place them into our categories, we have no chance of hearing any part of their music.

So, when I think of the range of cultural contexts in which Extrum-Fernandez has worked, I am reminded of how important local ministry, cultural skills, and micro practices truly are. These are not extras thrown in as helpful aids. They are central to justice ministry because they are central to the Incarnation and to the lives of flesh-and-blood people.

Follow the Trot Lines

Appointed to a program to build a ministry for the prison population and their families, Stanley E. Basler knew it was necessary to build connections and gather others to help. He immediately went around his annual conference to recruit volunteers, and he eventually had people signed up to work in every prison. Basler reports that most volunteers were conservatives.

It was important for him to establish his identity and credibility. He found that wearing a clerical collar was crucial, especially at the state capitol; the identity claimed with a collar was far better than being "a liberal Democrat" in his home state. Holding two theological degrees and trained as a lawyer, Basler kept his identity with the church. This helped him with the department of corrections. He also noted that it did *not* help his credibility when he later became a faculty member of a school of theology. The church was far more powerful with the prison system than the seminary.

In communication and working with the department of corrections, Basler constantly told them that he had similar interests and concerns in the work with the prison population and their families. He pointed out that many of the problems inmates and their families have cannot be solved by the government. This, he reminded them, is where the church can be of great help, especially in local communities where these ex-prisoners return to live. To do this work required building relationships while people were *in* prison and developing relationships with churches and people back in the communities before they returned there.

Advocacy, of course, was a crucial dimension of his prison work. In doing this work, Basler said, "Sometimes you have to go over people's heads to get things done." He illustrated this point with the guard at the gate of a prison who would use his power to keep Basler out. One of the people connected with a prison advised him: "Don't worry about the chain of command. You are a United Methodist minister; go over his head!" Of course, Basler understands that it is important to know when—and with whom—you can and cannot do this. He further advised that you must document your overtures to prison or state personnel before exceeding their authority. That is, Basler would send them emails making requests before he went over their heads. Typically, they did not respond to his communications. If they later confronted him about taking the issue to their supervisor, he had a paper trail of his unanswered requests. Basler also learned that using this sort of authoritative power gains respect when, before, you were perceived as powerlessness before the agents of the system. For example, the guard at the gate began to respect him after Basler went over his head.

He also found that there were limits to what he could do. For instance, he could not take up the cause of sex offenders in the context of the Oklahoma State legislature. It simply did not work. He also found that communications with legislators or state personnel had certain boundaries. A letter to them could not be too argumentative. It should not, he discovered, be in the negative. Rather, correspondence worked best when it described the problem as concretely as possible and then laid out what could be done. Further, he had to learn what words were a turn-off. Word choice was key, and biblical references needed to be foundational. For example, Basler found that legislators did not believe ex-offenders should have advocates. As a result, Basler changed his focus from advocacy for ex-offenders to protecting and benefiting society. He told legislators, "We both want society protected. We are common in our goals; we are just pursuing it through different means." This worked much better and allowed Basler to pursue his central concerns.

Basler then shifted in the interview and said, "You have to know how to run the trot lines." In fishing terms, a trot line is a long, strong line stretched across a stream of water with shorter pieces of string tied to it roughly equal distances from each other. The other ends of these short strings are fitted with baited hooks to catch fish. Basler used this phrase to speak of the connections of power at work in dealing with the state house and other power arrangements. Where is the trot line, the strength of power holding things together, and who are those smaller forms of power connected to this main source? Being able to work in these relationships and connections of power is essential to getting things done. He found that these power dynamics operated even within the department of corrections.

At one time in Basler's ministry, he was able to have some inmates attend church services outside the walls of the prison. Not long after that, a conservative Republican who did a lot of micromanaging became governor and immediately stopped allowing prisoners to go off center to churches, a policy that would have killed Basler's program. But the Speaker of the Oklahoma House was an active member of The United Methodist Church, and he insisted to Basler that this was not the governor's intention and put him in connection with a man who was close to the governor. So, Basler says, he learned that this trot line was run from The United Methodist Church to the Speaker to an influencer of the governor. He further acknowledges, "I really don't know if the governor ever actually got involved. All I know is that after the meeting with the influencer, the problem disappeared immediately." Knowing who had relationships with whom, knowing who had access, and knowing where and when to move were critical.

Glancing back through this interview section with Basler, there are crucial practices that stand out. His work at building connections for ministry and recruiting volunteers is quite extraordinary. Central to that and certainly to his work with the legislature was establishing his identity and credibility. Wearing a collar and having his identity with the church and not being seen as "a liberal Democrat" opened many doors. His continual communications with the department of corrections emphasized their common interest in helping ex-prisoners become good citizens when they return to local communities in Oklahoma. But he also learned the intricacies of advocacy, and part of that was developing the will and the skill to go over people's heads, which, as it turned out, were very important in the development and use of his own power. Finally, learning to work the relationships of power in politics and government—learning to run the trot lines—involved a range of practices, some of them as small as talking to the right person who knows the right person at the right time. Basler's political moves and working through relationships provide some indication of how micro practices build up to create macro consequences.

Stories and Power

Closely related to his discussion of the relationship between stories and culture was Billy Vaughan's discussion of the relationship between stories and power. Some years back, he read Walter Wink's books on the powers.[24] They made a lasting impression upon him. At that point he began to ask people to write their stories in relationship to Wink's work. That is, how did they experience authority and power and how did they interact with them?

At Memphis Theological Seminary—which he tells me is "50 percent non-White and 50 percent women, and a great population to work with"—they organize into small groups of no more than twelve. Each person tells his or her own story and its relationship to power. Vaughan reports that the clergy are not willing to be vulnerable in front of laypeople, so they work exclusively with the latter. He says this is "a great context for stories across race, class, and gender."

I think the power of stories will not surprise readers of this book. Putting the story of the world into the story of God is central to the work of ministry. In this sense, it is to tell a better story, indeed, a story that confronts the principalities and powers where God bats last.

Selling Ideas and Working with Angels

John Culp describes himself as a salesman of ideas. When Martin Luther King Jr. was killed, Culp was too afraid to go to the funeral. Instead, he continued his studies at Candler School of Theology and, unbeknownst to him, prepared for his life's work as an advocate for the Black community. While at Candler, he put his Clinical Pastoral Education to use as a chaplain at Grady Hospital, a hospital in the heart of Atlanta's Black community that had just recently been desegregated in 1965. The stories he heard from the patients changed and transformed him.

When he went home to South Carolina in the 1970s, he organized suburban youth to work with the Black community. Thus began a program of seventy thousand participants in forty-eight camps. In doing so, he learned from and worked with a wide range of mentors in his home state and beyond. He commented, "When you discover your values, every decision is based on a value." For instance, in every church he pastored, he found a nearby mental hospital and provided spiritual care to the patients. Seeing himself as a social activist, he liked to create things that involve people in justice work. For example, in Aiken, South Carolina, he created seminars in which participants visited a local federal nuclear site. This effort was a follow-up to a pastoral letter on nuclear weapons written by The United Methodist Council of Bishops. This seminar raised the consciousness of its attendees about the processes by which these weapons were made and the magnitude of nuclear waste involved. Culp reports that nuclear site now has thousands of gallons of waste without any way to dispose of it. People also learned of the levels of destruction caused by these devices. They became conversant with treaties regarding nuclear weapons, and some of his people became nuclear pacifists because of the seminar. Since 90 percent of his church people worked at the site, that could have been a problem. "But," he says, "if you are a pastor, your people will love you."

In Greenville, he worked with inner-city youth and faced head-on the issues of alcoholism and drug abuse. In Gifford, three Roman Catholic nuns wanted a presence in the poor community, so he joined them and brought together young people to design a camp to work on poverty homes. On St. Helena Island, Culp recruited one hundred kids in the summer to work at Penn Center, an African American cultural and educational center built on the campus of one of the nation's first schools for formerly enslaved people. He says, “Churches turned lemons into lemonade and made ministry happen.”

Culp got involved with LGBTQ+ rights while working with others to address AIDS and also by voting as a delegate to The United Methodist General Conference to make the UMC more welcoming.

He helped United Methodists in Malawi build a church, and he visited Africa University in Mutare, Zimbabwe, calling the school “one of the best things in the world we have going in the UMC.” In another example, he put together fifty-one stories of people who participated in Salkehatchie Summer Service, a program and outreach effort that sends volunteers to repair the homes of the poor. Each summer, one million dollars in construction costs and supplies are spent to update two hundred homes by this program. Seventy thousand campers have participated in this effort in the forty-five years of its existence, and more than six thousand families have been helped by these repairs.

Culp told me, “I like to be a social artist and see a plan come together. I am mystical and spiritual and believe in angels. At the start of Salkehatchie, a house fire killed three small children. The Black father asked me to do the funeral. On reflection, this Black man was an angel.” Culp believes God opens closed doors, and he sees angels as instrumental in breaking down the walls of exclusion in the church and the world. In assessing his approach, he comes up with ideas and gets others to do the work. Operating with a basic intuition, he can assess in meetings where people are and what they are prepared to do. Serving as a catalyst, he identifies this as “where the mystical comes in. Things happen, they jump out at you.” This enables him to know how to move and with whom to collaborate. He concluded, "If we do not believe in surprises, we do not believe in God."

What do you do with a clergyman like Culp? He sells ideas, he gets people involved in exposure to a nuclear site and its ecological threat and destructive capacities, works with inner-city youth and children on alcoholism and drugs, cooperates with Catholic nuns to upgrade homes for those in poverty, develops work camps all over South Carolina where churches turn lemons into lemonade, kind of like turning water into wine. He builds relationships with LGBTQ+ people and addresses AIDS, and his concern has an international relationship with Malawi and Africa University. The sheer macro scale of the work he initiates and attends is mind-boggling. At the same time, these projects all begin in micro practices like being a catalyst, selling ideas, and meeting with individuals and small groups. He believes in angels, and his one-on-ones with them result in some very large programs. Meanwhile, he works out of a basic intuition and comes up with ideas and gets others to do the work. He sees all of this as mystical, where "things happen" and "they jump out at you." For him, surprises are simply a direct outgrowth of believing in God.

Doing Change Through Community Organization

Jose L. Palos remembers the first time he encountered community organizing, when he invited a pro–union farmworker event to meet in his church.

A pastor in San Antonio at the time, he became acquainted with Communities Organized for Public Service (COPS), the originating organization of the Industrial Areas Foundation (IAF) work in San

Antonio. COPS was initially Roman Catholic, Palos informs me, but then they began The Metro Alliance (METRO), which was a more Protestant organization actively in collaboration with COPS. From that time forward, San Antonio and Palos would never be the same.[25]

The day following the farmworker meeting, a lay leader in his church asked him what authorized him to have that meeting in the church. Palos answered that *The Book of Discipline* of the UMC—the official book outlining the law, doctrine, administration, organizational work, and procedures of The United Methodist Church—allows the pastor to do that. "I have that authority," he told the lay leader. "I am able to have those kinds of meetings." Palos said that people will take away your authority if you don't take a stand, but it is important to claim legitimate rules and procedures. Palos then stated that the positive impact of his taking rightful authority was that that lay leader who questioned him became a good friend and a supporter of the organizing work.

Palos had served in San Antonio back in the late sixties. When he returned there in 2002, he could see the great change that had occurred in the West Side community because of the organizing work of COPS/METRO. He saw improvements in city lighting, in street repair, in drainage of flood waters, in trash pickup, and in the schools. Before that time, people in this area were ignored and neglected, but when the school board took a school tax issue to the Supreme Court, they won! Things changed.

At this point in our interview, Palos began a description of his work that reflected the cycle of organizing used by the IAF. He first told me how important it was to have one-on-one meetings with people in his congregation and in the larger community. As I have indicated before, the one-on-one is the basic building block of community organizing. These are thirty-minute meetings in which someone from the organizing effort deliberately meets with another person to discern whether they are a good candidate to join the work. The initiator of the conversation mainly listens to discover the passion, the self-interest broadly conceived, the energy, and the readiness of this potential member. The entire structure and work of broad-based organizing is built on the one-on-one.

Palos met with people in his congregation, people in the community, city officials, and others involved in community organizing. Palos found that some of his congregational leaders were initially resistant, but through active work in one-on-ones and participation in other practices of the organizing cycle, real change happened in his congregation. He spoke of house meetings, power analyses and research actions, civic academies, public actions, and evaluations—the key ingredients of the organizing cycle.

Palos spoke appreciatively of one organizer with whom he worked closely. Every time the pastors met, Palos remembers, an organizer who happened to be a former priest brought an article that "related social issues to our concerns in the community, which we then as a group of pastors discussed." This organizer also brought theological articles that provided Palos and other pastors with the "background and the connections between faith and organizing and the issues we faced in the community." He expressed regret that the next organizer continued to bring articles about organizing and social issues but not about theology and did not engage the group in theological reflection.

Palos moved to another church in the city that was not involved in COPS/METRO, but he was able to get them engaged through one-on-ones and other aspects of the organizing cycle. For instance, they had candidate forums where COPS/METRO invited candidates to speak to the issues of importance to the community organization. Rather than give political speeches, the candidates were asked explicit questions from the leadership of the community organization about where they stood on certain issues and what they would support if they were elected to office. The key point is that his congregational members developed self-confidence when they saw people like themselves asking questions and even confronting the candidates.

Palos also emphasized the importance of going into the neighborhoods and knocking on doors to find out what the people really needed. He says that people who opened their doors were surprised that church people would ask about their needs. As a result, some came to church seeking membership, while others came for food and for clinical services that provided blood pressure screenings, nutrition, and preventive care education.

Meanwhile, all these things fed back into the church. It affected Palos's sermons because his preaching connected the faith with the work going on in the community. In his prayers he would remember people, organizations, and events and ask for their needs to be met and for people to be blessed. In Bible class he would make connections between the scripture and what was going on in the community. All these became ways to connect with people's lives. He remembers particularly one woman who would always raise questions in Bible study, which opened doors for consideration of the circumstances going on in the community.

During the interview, he recalled a teaching from a seminary professor about managing conflict and building consensus. After telling a story about a previous pastor who almost had a fist fight with a parishioner over a disagreement, the professor said that you must work with the representative small groups in the church and that the church board always needs representatives from these small groups. Making decisions and building consensus requires careful work in the small groups of the church so that by the time an issue gets to the board for discussion and decision, the consensus has virtually been reached, or, at least, a large group of people has been in on the discussion and is informed. More than that, when a decision is reached under these circumstances, not only will it not be a problem for the board, but implementation of it will be far easier.

There were also small group discussions and meetings with clergy where those present talked about their neighborhoods, their needs and visions, and their faith. Further, Palos would visit with people who came to the food pantry, talking with them one-on-one. He would ask, "Do you want me to pray with you?" Many of these people, of course, were not related to the church, but this became a way for him to connect with them. Palos stated, "These were small things people didn't notice, but I was doing this persistently. I wanted to know where people were hurting and to try to respond."

To conclude this report of my interview with Palos, let me say a word about my general impression of the interview with him. I had trouble following him at times because he would move from one practice of the organizing cycle to another while I was still back taking notes on the former. He seemed to move seamlessly from one part of that cycle to another, and I would often stop him to get clarity and make sure I understood what he was saying. My point is that he is so formed by a cycle of organizing that it has become formative of who he is. He embodies the cycle.

Synergy

Marlon Tilghman came prepared to our interview with an outline of micro practices in his justice ministry. He began by indicating that he must have a passion, something on his heart. He must have skin in the game, and he reminded me that the scripture tells us not to grow weary in well doing.

After that, he spoke of one-on-one meetings and the need to find synergy from those. By synergy, I took him to mean occasions when a combination of things creates greater force or impact than their individual effects could ever have done alone. None of the other interviewees had quite indicated that dynamic in the one-on-one. According to Tilghman, "Once you develop these one-on-ones so that you have a good core team of five to seven people, then you have people connected to family and to people at both the personal and public level." This comment shows that micro practices at the one-on-one level become public in impact through organizing and other macro practices.

Tilghman made it clear that he doesn't know it all and is always looking for what he doesn't know. For this reason, he is slow to speak in meetings and slow to act. He watches out for babble: people who just talk, people who have opinions but don't act, and people who fill the air with words but don't organize.

Yet he knows that language matters. Changing the dominant narrative through the skillful use of words is important. During the last legislative session in Maryland, a bill was stalled because their organizing efforts couldn't get the legislature to understand what they were talking about. They were working on a bill to define and limit "*juvenile* interrogation." The language did not work with the legislators. Tilghman reports that juvenile interrogation seemed to imply "juvenile delinquency," a phrase that the opponents were able to weaponize politically. So, they changed the name to "*child* interrogation," which changed the perception and lead to the passage of the legislation. While opponents continued to attempt to use "juvenile interrogation," they were not successful. He was the only pastor, but the coalition comprised Jews for Justice and Catholic Charities—both lay organizations—plus secular groups like the ACLU and the unions. This successful action illustrates his comment about synergy.

Tilghman also emphasized the importance of legwork. Getting down on the ground, meeting with, talking with, and organizing allies is essential. At the same time, he said, "After the meetings, when we are done with all our legwork, I'm going to do some 'knee work.'"

Here he commented about how things change over the course of working for justice during the timeline of a single issue. "The climate changes," he notes, so it's necessary to stay on top of what is going on. Power holders must be monitored continually; it is necessary to stay in touch and know who the players are.

Part of this staying in touch with change requires close relationships with one's own supporters in the organizing effort. Tilghman observes that people have their own networks that can be very important. One church in their organizing group, for example, had a senator as a member of the congregation. People from the senator's church began writing him letters and dropping notes on his desk. The influence of these members of his own faith community grew out of existing relationships.

Tilghman then quoted one of the major aphorisms of broad-based community organizing, "We have no permanent enemies and no permanent allies." Keeping the door open and looking for new ways to work together, even with previous opponents, can work for the public good.

That he was also well acquainted with the political enterprise came through in our conversation when he said, "Be flexible, be prepared to compromise, but be strong." During the time of the legislative session when we had our interview, the legislature had tabled one of the bills his organization supported. "We told them we would be back in 2023. These legislators had told us that they supported our proposed legislative change. We are going to be back and to push."

This case had to do with child cases being adjudicated in adult court but then being kicked back down to juvenile court. Tilghman's organization asked, "Why go to adult court at all? It's a waste of time and money." He pointed out that in juvenile court, you can prevent youth from repeating criminal activity. Interventions can be made to move youth in a more positive direction. Tilghman tells me that on the first try to make the legislation better, the legislature actually made it worse, including ten-, eleven-, and twelve-year-olds under the purview of the adult court, but he is clear that his group will continue to press the issue until a better result is achieved.

His final word was, "Come across as powerful. If you come across as weak, they disregard you. Hold fast, take action, play the long game. And don't give up power."

After our interview, it seemed so right that Tilghman had emphasized synergy from the get-go. One could read his interview as the pulling together of a host of practices that increase the impact of any one of them taken alone. His own passion and heat and skin in the game; the one-on-one as an ongoing lived practice; developing connections and working with people, a finesse with language, the combination of legwork and "knee work," staying in touch with the movement and relations of an issue; the impermanence of allies and enemies; not forgetting the connections of supporters, being able to compromise but thereby to claim strength: the synergetic impact of such practices when they become the habitus of one's life is incalculable in its impact and witness.

The Power of the One-on-One

Joseph W. Daniels Jr. began his interview stating, "The power of the one-on-one meeting continues to be the foundation of getting anything done." In fact, he says that he spends 70 percent of his time meeting with people to discover their "self-interest, their vision, their passion, and their interest for the work of the Lord." He sets up meetings with people, has conversations with them, and then asks who else should he talk to.

He observes that this model comes from Jesus, who had a core group of perhaps three, the larger group of twelve disciples, and then as many as 120 others. Noting that we often strive to be mega churches, he contends that if we follow Christ, we can make "the colossal church." He concludes, "That's what we do. It's that simple." It is an investment of time and energy in relationship change. He points out further that we must continually change—there is always turnover in the work of the church, so you must constantly get to know new people.

In one-on-ones, Daniels is always looking for common threads or themes. "If I talk to you and you with me, and then I talk with Mr. Johnson, Ms. Smith, and Mr. Hayes across town, and you all begin to share the same passion or theme or themes, then I know where people are. I think I also get some idea of where God is, and I begin to discern places to get traction." One of the themes he has found is that "people like the neighborhood but are afraid they may be displaced." They want to stay in the neighborhood, so Daniels will then ask them, "What does Jesus want you to do?"

After significant numbers of one-on-one conversations, the next step is the house meeting. Here he follows the community organizing model known as the cycle of organizing.[26] In that cycle, the house meeting is the gathering of a larger group of people. In these get-togethers they often break up into smaller groups with a convener and a note taker. The conversation then occurs around central interests, passions, themes, and stories. These discussions are then reported back to the larger group, and the building of a consensus is begun. At this point in the interview, Daniels referred to Nehemiah, who walked the streets with the people and encouraged their passion to rebuild Jerusalem.

Daniels went on to talk more about the one-on-ones and to break down how he went about creating connections with people through relational meetings. He usually asks, "Where are you from?" He then advises that you have to keep people talking and listen, listen, listen. Daniels will continue to ply people with questions about how they got to the place where they are. He will ask them to tell a story and continue to pursue stories from them. At the right time, he asks them what they would like to see the community become. He wants to know how they can create life together.

The Dialectic of the One-on-One

Angelique Mason said, "I believe everything we need is in the house," meaning that a church or a community organization already has the capacities and skills in the people there to do the work. The problem, she suggests, is that "we don't always ask about the talents and the skills people have." The one-on-one, she claims, is a good way to get in touch with these capacities.

In doing one-on-ones, she attempts to meet people where they are and then go to the next level. "I just ask people what their skills and talents are," she said. "I don't dance around. I just get to the point." She recognizes that sometimes she's too direct, so she has some other practices she uses. For one thing, she prays and asks God to reveal to her how she needs to approach someone and what she needs to do. She also watches body language, looks people in the eye, and considers the way people avoid you or are simply not comfortable around you. Paying attention to people's language is important, especially when they say yes. She wants to make sure they really mean it, because she doesn't have time for "shucking and jiving."

At the same time, she admits that sometimes she's too analytical and has to make sure she doesn't offend someone. So, she will try to find a comfortable space where people can be free to express themselves. She tries to be careful not to tell them they were wrong for acting or speaking in a certain way in a given setting. Instead, she will simply ask them what happened.

In these kinds of interactions, she says that one-on-ones are the mortar that holds things together. In relational meetings, she works to give space to do what's required, and says, "You must remember that you're not here to make everybody happy." She seals this point by remembering that Jesus "called people out." Again, however, she warns that you cannot micromanage, that you must give people space and let them make mistakes. She understands that you can make a task harder when you could've made it easier, that sometimes we have to say, "Let's go [together] and get this done."

She tries to remember that "everybody is valuable and has something to bring to the table." She often reminds herself that you must love people to work with them. "We claim to show the love of God," she notes, "which means that we have to be concerned about them." She gets it that sometimes she has "to agitate people," but in the name of that same love, she "must not shut them down."

She never tells people to lift themselves up by their bootstraps. Some of the people she works with don't have boots. Instead, she works to find ways to open doors. She says in this connection that she finds people "don't want handouts, but rather hands up."

She's also clear, "I don't have a script. I do one person at a time. I assess the need, and I also try to determine what each person brings to the table." Further, she asks what she and that person have in common. "We are all human, just different. I want to understand a person's culture and their family," she says. When I ask how she does this, she said that she has a sense of humor and uses that to get them laughing. She finds that "a lot of truth can be told in a joke." And that a lot of good can come from making people comfortable.

Mason has been in ministry for more than thirty years, with only the last fifteen as a pastor. Previously, she was an administrator for three different churches, a position she chose because she thought people were more honest with church staff than with the minister. At one point, however, her presiding elder (a supervisor over several churches in the AME denomination) told her, "You have helped to grow three churches; it is now time you become a pastor." God had called her to preach.

I asked what keeps her going, and her answer was instant: "*People.* I get joy from people, especially when they climb out of what's holding them down." Further, she informed me, "When we are exposed to different experiences, we learn what's out there." She moves then directly to the Bible, to scripture as story, reporting that she is a storyteller, and that the Bible is her manual. Yet she also works with people of other faith traditions. In doing interfaith work, she doesn't always refer to God by that name but uses the concept of "a higher power."

I was impressed by how Mason kept a "dialectic" going throughout our interview. Just a cursory reading of her comments above reveals practices of meeting people where they are, but then going to the next level. She doesn't dance around; she gets to the point. But she realizes she can be too direct, so she uses practices of prayer, of noticing body language, of looking people in the eye, of finding comfortable spaces to talk, of helping people to express themselves, of refraining from telling them they are wrong. She understands that she can be too analytical, but she must not offend people. There are times to agitate, but not to shut people down. People will make mistakes, but she must not micromanage. She is clearly centered in the stories of Jesus, but she works in interfaith settings and speaks of a higher power. I suppose someone could read these as a list of contradictions, but I see them as descriptive of the moves of an astute practitioner naming skills that go into the effective work of one-on-ones.

Porta Potties, Chaos, Confrontation, and Stabilization

Doing change sometimes requires disruption, or at least the *threat* of disruption. You have already met John Flowers and the ministry he had with the homeless at Travis Park UMC in San Antonio. He tells of a time when the city locked up the public rest rooms, presenting a serious problem for the homeless people. Flowers told the people at City Hall that he was going to order ten porta potties, have them placed there in front of the building, and that they were going to have a "shit-in" at City Hall. The threat was sufficient. While they never did host this protest, they did get a couple of porta potties for the homeless in Travis Park as a concession from City Hall.

Using threats, of course, is a risky business. For one thing, a threat must be credible if it is to be effective.[27] Flowers had developed considerable credibility on things like this. He is a physically imposing man, over six feet tall and weighing more than two hundred pounds. He also has a high tolerance for risk and loves chaos.

In the time that Flowers was at Travis Park UMC, Donde Ashmos Plowman and associates used complexity and chaos theory to study the leadership styles of the congregation. Calling the congregation "Mission Church," they found that the leaders "destabilized the organization by creating and highlighting conflict and 'embracing uncertainty.'" From this they drew several conclusions that we can only briefly report in this space, so I recommend a full reading of their article.[28]

Among their findings were several dynamics important for our study. They discovered that these leaders tended not so much to initiate innovation themselves, but rather to encourage others to do so. The leaders did more to interpret change than to create it, and they "manage words rather than manage people." For example, in their use of language, they often asked people, "What would Jesus do?" or "What does unconditional love require?"

Plowman and her researchers also emphasized the importance of a stabilizing force. Flowers operated as a co-pastor with his spouse, Karen Vannoy, whose gifts and skills complemented those of her husband. With a different management style, she was far better at detail work and planning. The researchers found that she was "the stabilizing factor" and "the cerebral type." Flowers, they concluded, was more like "the giant Labrador." Together, they made an extraordinary team.

6

DOING CHANGE, PART 2

Bridge Builder Versus Rabble Rouser

Michael Zedek said he is "more bridge builder than rabble rouser," someone more aware of the common ground people share than what divides them. He reflected back to 1976, when he began his friendship with Emanuel Cleaver, later Congressman Cleaver, whom we will meet in chapter 10. "Cleaver invited me to preach, and we built a connection. Our choirs were in each other's place of worship, and we had other reasons to be together. We knew that contention did not have to be the final word, and the two of us convened a group to do bridge building."

Zedek then told several stories that displayed his approach to bridge building. When he was in rabbinical school in Cincinnati, he became involved with local farmworkers. This happened, he said, "because the organizer needed someone to talk to, and so I talked to him." The farmworkers at that time used a tactic in which they would go into a grocery store and load up a cart with non-union grapes. When they went to the checkout line, they told the checkout person that they did not realize they were non-union grapes and would then leave their cart and the grapes there for the employee to replace on the shelves. Zedek supported the goals of the farmworkers but said, "I could not bear putting the work back on the people who did not own the store, so I helped the employee return the grapes to the shelf."

Next, he told a story about the now-deceased Fred Phelps, an anti-gay activist known for his slogan, "God hates fags." Zedek reminded me that Phelps began by targeting Jews, then gay people, and then back to Jews because that got more attention. Zedek was rabbi of a congregation in Chicago when he caught wind that Phelps was organizing a demonstration outside of his synagogue. Zedek was advised by the Jewish defense organizations to just to ignore Phelps. But he could not do that. His congregation included a retired rabbi and members who were Holocaust survivors. So, he sent out an email to local Christian clergy saying, "This is not my fight." The Christian pastors motivated their congregants to help, and when the day came for Phelps's demonstration at the synagogue, Zedek had nine hundred people; Phelps had five.

Without any transition, Zedek then discussed Aaron and Moses, noting that the Hebrew Bible "presents them as brothers because their leadership styles are totally different." Moses was close to God but had difficulty relating to people, while Aaron had difficulty relating to God but was close to the people. Zedek sees them on a continuum, but then admitted that he understands Aaron better than Moses: "If I were not aware of it, I could not go beyond it." He then added, seemingly as a point of instruction for any priest, minister, or rabbi, "Aaron is the high priest but he's not better than anyone else."

I was intrigued by Zedek's assertion that the Hebrew Bible presents Aaron and Moses as brothers *because* their leadership styles are totally different. His use of the word "because" struck me. I have not been able to get it out of my mind for the simple reason that it is such an important way to think of brotherhood. (Zedek would also be quick to use "sisterhood" in other situations.) Aaron and Moses were brothers *because* they had different leadership styles. It is a kind of equation of brotherhood (and sisterhood) with difference, a claim that can be made without denying similarities among brothers and sisters. In part, Zedek is making the case that it is appropriate for some to be bridge builders and others to be rabble rousers. Yet these were representative notions for Zedek. There is a range of roles in justice work, and these roles are to be appreciated and employed. Sometimes a fight is not your fight and must be taken up by others.

In cases like these, I try to grasp the mass of micro practices that go into each aspect of Zedek's characterizations. It is easy to gloss over his one-on-one meetings with Cleaver and other meetings with his own congregation in developing the relationship between his synagogue and Cleaver's church. I also think of his talks with the farmworker's organizer and the fruitfulness of those conversations. I cannot help but wonder about the response of a check-out counter employee to a rabbi who helps that person replace the items used, quite obviously, for protest purposes and to make a point. Zedek cared about farmworkers, but he also cared about grocery store employees. Bridge builders do that.

Feeding Two Birds with One Worm

Mark Matheny spoke of two sets of practices that he regarded as very helpful in doing justice ministry. The first was using music, sports, art, and literature to establish common ground with people and express the themes of the gospel. The second set of practices were formed around the law of multiple utility, that is, finding things that advance the general good on several levels at once. Matheny recalled the old proverb about killing two birds with one stone; he changed that to a proverb of his own, "Feeding two birds with one worm." Mark gave an example of church members and friends who had construction skills and were interested in volunteering with Habitat for Humanity. He encouraged them to go through the training and serve the organization, then to be available for disaster response work through their United Methodist annual conference, then to participate in an ongoing justice concern for other housing, then to share presentations about these experiences with Sunday school classes and other groups, all the while keeping spiritual blessings and gaining wonderful friendships. "Now that's multiple utility!" Matheny exclaimed.

Matheny then mentioned several other practices that he regularly uses. From his father, he learned the value of cheerleading, the importance of rooting for and encouraging people in their talents, abilities, and actions. For instance, when he learned that one of his church members loved to act, Matheny worked with him to put together a brief performance in which Matheny played Barnabas the encourager while the layman had the main role of Paul the leader. In that same church, some men presented a Last Supper drama, but the women were left out. So they worked up a play called "Women of the Bible."

Their play began to alternate each year with the men's Maundy Thursday production.

Matheny noted, "Sometimes you are lucky." And strategically, one must "tap into that." He spoke of befriending and networking with one man who came to Memphis and became a public defender. He and Matheny got to be friends and began to explore the political possibilities for him in the city. He would later become County Mayor and then City Mayor. Still active as a lawyer, he has helped to develop Black-owned businesses in the community.

I was intrigued, too, that once again that element of etiquette or patterns of hospitality came in to play in Matheny's interview. He spoke specifically of the Southern pattern of friendship, of introducing an acquaintance and being able to rely on such connections to initiate the organizing of a relatively small, informal group, but one that could play a very important role when later combined with other such groups. Even so, he remarked, "Anything can establish a conversation with someone, an idea, a problem, or something for the community."

Matheny also joined many other interviewees in warning of the danger of micromanagement. Delegation, mutuality in decision making, and shared work by a team are crucial. Along with this, "You have to realize where you are not strong, and you must delegate." He remembered working with the Highland Area Renewal Corporation. They were working with ten neighborhoods, and they needed a detail person. They found a woman who served as secretary/treasurer of the group, and she was the perfect fit. He had observed earlier that introversion can make tough barriers for ministry, but in this case, her introversion and her capacity for working with particulars coincided with and utilized her inward orientation. On another issue, they needed an independent transportation network cheaper than Uber to take people to work or to doctor's appointments. Again, a detail-oriented person was needed, and she emerged.

Look back briefly at the micro practices Matheny suggested, especially the importance of using music, sports, art, and literature to establish common ground; as well as the practice of multiple utility, of feeding two birds with one worm. He also emphasized the value of cheerleading. His approach to power, especially that of city leaders, takes seriously the need to find common interests as the beginning of a relationship. He also mentioned luck, and surely that cannot be ruled out. Further, he realizes the role of etiquette, hospitality, and Southern patterns of friendship as part of the culture in which he works. Finally, he recognizes that micromanagement is to be rejected, that recognition of one's weaknesses is crucial, and that delegation is required. Matheny's interview revealed a pastor well acquainted with his Southern context. He has mastered practices that enable him to move and create change even in circumstances where the options are limited and directions are constrained. Once again, the small things we do find ways to do justice.

Doing Change with Left-Wing Radicals

David Carl Olson emphasized the importance of recognizing congregation members for the work they do in the world. "Pay attention to their work out in the field beyond the church. Note their contributions, and recognize these in sermons, church news columns, and in conversations." He said it is important to use the language of leadership, that is, to recognize people as *leaders,* not only as activists.

He then gave me an example of a practice he has used for some time in various forms. Almost twenty years ago, he served the Unitarian Universalist Community Church of Boston, a congregation filled with old radicals that had a long history in the pursuit of justice. Olson's fear, however, was that they would "hold up the bright torch of justice and not see the shadow behind them."

The congregation had a tradition of conversation after the sermon on Sunday morning. He proposed to the Sunday Services Committee that they allot seven minutes on Sunday morning *before* the sermon so someone could speak to "the condition of the congregation." He had the names of five or six people who wanted to address the gathering, and so he prepared.

And he was surprised. They did this for five years, and "not one time did someone jump into the pulpit and act out with accusations." Rather, it was "action-driven interrogation." The speakers told their stories, talked about their spirituality, and indicated what they wanted to pass on to the future. "It was some of the richest work I ever experienced," said Olson. One old activist, who typically called for an action a week, used his seven minutes to say, "My church is not a political party; my church is bigger than that. We are not a partisan place, but a human place, a place trying to make the world better."

The idea for the seven-minute addresses occurred in a conversation Olson had with a young member of the congregation who loved the topics discussed after the sermon but had problems with cantankerous people. "I invited her to get up and share the kind of church she wanted to be a part of. It put it in my head that other people would want to do the same thing."

At this point in our interview, Olson turned to the cheerleader role of a minister, telling several stories about the importance of empowering the congregation to shape its worship and work in the world. He used a story from the First Unitarian Church in Baltimore. This congregation had a long and distinguished history but was struggling with their justice ministry. It manifested itself in two characteristics. First, the congregation was bureaucratic, and their justice work was that of a central clearing house, not a ministry as such. Second, they spent a lot of time in that committee giving permission to people to do things. Olson saw that they needed to be more spontaneous.

A Peace and Justice Ministry leadership team was created to commission projects that could be done in the name of the congregation's ministry. They dealt with serving food to the homeless, with working on housing and schools, with helping bring children out of poverty, and with creating a legislative agenda. Leaders from these projects would then meet with Olson each month to talk about what was going on. There were also people the church wanted to give a voice but were not structured into the church—the homeless, for example. In talking with these groups and at their suggestion, the church turned over its Parish Hall and Education wing to those working with unhoused people. Together they planned a weekend to address food insecurity, other needs, and social services in one room. That way services and community could all be part of the work. This happened, Olson said, "because I was able to listen to those sidelined so that we were a community." He further explained that the social justice committee didn't seem real until they had this new organizational aspect of social ministry. For others who wanted to be engaged in ministry with people in need, this allowed for more spontaneity and for the expression of their interests in a capacity for change while being with people in need in the process.

Olson then talked about another issue in Boston where they worked on conditions in the public schools. In this situation, he often found himself in front of a microphone before of a crowd. But he believed that the teachers themselves needed to make the case. So he gave reporters the names of teachers he knew would be good spokespeople, and he stepped out of the limelight. He wanted the teachers at the center of attention and at the front edge of the action. This was important, he suggested, because when the time came for them to go to City Hall for negotiations, "we needed the teachers to sit at the bargaining table." Further, "To give public testimony is good; it's good for people to speak from their lives, their hearts."

For some pastors, surely, ministry with a bunch of left-wing radicals would seem like a holiday. But people of any political persuasion can become bureaucratic, controlling, and set in their ways. Olson offers practices for addressing circumstances of this kind, such as the importance of paying attention to people who hold leadership positions beyond the congregation, and especially to calling the attention of others in the church to them; the skillful ways he praised the past and was a cheerleader for the present; his willingness to offer up the pulpit to church members and how well they responded and performed in the work they began together; how he pulled together volunteers and recipients of services and helped them become a community; and his good sense that teachers needed to be their own leaders, and that playing that out trained them and prepared them for demonstrations and negotiations at City Hall. I think of the conversations, the telephone calls, the thank-you cards, the pats on the back, the expressions of appreciation for the presentations of the laity, the humility of getting out of the limelight, and more: all these things have not only interactive force, but cumulative impact. This kind of mutuality builds an ethos—establishes healthy, faithful practices—and opens the door for emergent events of another and higher order.

He was clear that he knew failure, and that "victories don't make up for the failures." He said, "I need to spend time with me, to see how this reflects who I am." He wanted to be clear, transparent with himself. To do that, he said, "I need to have a prayer life. I need the rudder to steer this work."

His last comment was, "Why the hell am I doing this?" I understood him to mean that he wants to get away from the huge causes that don't truly relate to one's life, the ones that become distractions from the causes that do. He's committed to organizing for action with down-on-the-ground people in a church and a community with causes related to their real lives and to the real lives of their children and grandchildren. To be sure, big issues get dealt with in church and community. In fact, they are probably better addressed this way when the ideas, the vitality, the vision, and the sense of the common good come from the ground up.

Alchemy

At the very heart of Marti Scott's ministry is a connection with church-based organizing. She often considers how Bible stories inform what we do, and she identifies passages that match different skill sets. She adds that in preaching, she doesn't talk about theology and spirituality without tying them to what's going on in people's lives.

She tells me that there are great leaders in the scripture, and that she will often ask her congregation and community people, "How are you a great leader?" It is evident, too, that Scott explores the capacities and skill sets of people in the church and the community, asking the question of how these can be used. For example, her church successfully organized to get the city to install a needed stop sign. This small start helped build their confidence to take on more.

Next, she told me about a combined project of her church, Euclid Avenue UMC, and their sister church just east of them, Olivet UMC, in a Chicago neighborhood. Behind the Olivet church is an empty lot where nothing had been going on for decades. So, they decided to put a garden on it. This meant they had to use the skill sets that people already had. First, they just needed to clean up the place. "We got garden boxes and beautified it," making it attractive, she said. As the garden began to take shape, they held vaccine clinics on the site and "brought people and kids together to get it done." It was, she said, "a racially diverse group, but doing it together consecrated it for the neighborhood." One of the kids told her, "Garden today and a playground tomorrow." Scott noted that a comment like that is important in their neighborhood.

Scott's next topic was "the free refrigerator." This project began by putting an empty refrigerator in the parking lot of the church. The idea was that people fill it when they had an abundance of food so that others can come and get the food they need. It was a twenty-four-hour food pantry, but different from "the old way" in which the church or another charitable organization had control, set limits on what a recipient could have, and determined which items they would get. Speaking to this, Scott asserted, "You don't have to be ashamed because you're poor. We wanted people to take what they needed."

They also needed partners, which included a suburban alliance, people in Oak Park, and a bank. While they all went in together, the church did the lion's share of the work. They also had a problem: COVID set in, and people were hungry. But they had a community. "We decided to bless the refrigerator." People who had never gone to church came out to bless this new, cool offering in the neighborhood.

Was it abused? Of course. On occasion, someone would take everything. But the next day, Scott says, "We would fill it up again." They believe that the people who take food really need it and that they took it because they were hungry. Of course, the church did need some education about this among themselves, such as learning to unpack bulk items so that people don't take everything. "Don't leave everything in one carton. Unpack it."

She then noted that justice work needs to be *fun*. "Fun brings out the energy and creativity. It manifests the creative powers of God and brings out wisdom, even as it loosens the brain." One expression of this fun was when they got their alderman to help pick up garbage. To get his attention, Scott and her group took garbage and put it in a street intersection, in this context a fun thing to do. Then having the alderman come to help and pick it up, surely not something at the top of his priorities, brought smiles and amusement to the work.

Such events as these help people understand the concept of power. Scott is convinced that there are a lot of ways to gain power without abusing it. Central to this, of course, is making allies. Her congregation works with community organizing going on in the area, which she characterized as "mom and pop community organizing" in contrast to the more corporate kinds. She added that "connecting with this kind of organizing work is a form of evangelism." She told a story of working with a community organizer when they stayed up all night planning events. The organizer had been a Roman Catholic priest before he got married and left the church. Working in organizing, he started thinking about the church differently and how it influenced the values of people. He realized how the values of religious upbringing had shaped him for organizing, and with that recognition, he began showing back up for church.

Scott understands that community organizing is using the church, but she thinks that's okay. It helps make connections with the community, and it's good for the church. The relationship of the church to organizing is not exploitation of one by the other but a mutual undertaking that enriches both. She closed her comments about organizing by reporting that one of the organizers now presents at a class Scott teaches at Garrett-Evangelical Theological Seminary.

Scott then moved to a different subject, one I did not connect immediately with her previous comments, but that took on increasing gravity as she continued to speak. She said, "A subtle but big thing is to teach people to be conscious of the demonic practice of shame, the shame that can be carried into the future, into the remainder of your life." She became autobiographical, "I grew up poor, and my father was an alcoholic who was often absent. We lived in a small town, and everybody knew your business. You are made to feel that you can't do it, that you can't make it, that there's something wrong with you."

"The image of the poor that people have," she continued, "is that the poor are dirty and lack hygiene." She told the story of a remark made to her by another student in graduate school who said, "You cannot have been poor, your teeth are too white." Remembering that moment, she said, "It is true that I was seventeen years old before I saw a dentist. So you feel inferior. You hear the name calling." She remembers, "My family fled Alabama after World War II searching for jobs. We lived in these three-room flats, places called 'Hillbilly Heaven.' Yet no one ever said that it was a wealthy guy who owned the house and never fixed it up." Scott offered, "In my case, had it not been for the UMC, those pastors, and the demands they placed on education, I would have been lost. I went to Garrett-Evangelical Theological Seminary and then to Northwestern to get a PhD. Without those I would not have made it."

Scott has also made use of musicals. On two occasions she has given a sermon series on the four characters in *The Wizard of Oz*, discussing their spirituality and how their contexts changed how they perceived the life of the wizard. The first time, seventeen years ago, she used the traditional *Wizard of Oz*. "This was community building on a spiritual level. I was making the point that some of us come at it academically (the Scarecrow); some as worker bees: Jesus was a carpenter, labor is good, organized (the Tin Man); others are prophetic and courageous leaders (the Lion); and, lastly, the mystics (Dorothy)." Scott offered, "I would argue social mystics and practical mystics imagine the new heaven on earth and do it. By listening and learning from one another, we become beloved community we learn to be more thoughtful, fuller hearted, courageous and visionary."

More recently, she used the African American retelling of the story, *The Wiz*, in her sermon series. In this version, when Dorothy encounters the scarecrow, he's up on a cross, and she cannot understand why he's not down. In Scott's sermon, the chorus comes in at this point to inform the audience that "the game is rigged and hopeless." She says, "After study, reparations, I felt like there was something we missed the first time we did it. *The Wiz* is deeper, truer, richer than the Wizard of Oz."

About five years ago, her church put on a performance they called "Rewriting the West Side Story." This presentation attempted to make the case for seeing Austin Avenue and Oak Park as the meeting place, rather than the dividing line, in the city. Austin Avenue separates Chicago's poorest and least-resourced African American community from Oak Park, which is diverse but still culturally White and upper middle class.

As I listened to her, I kept thinking to myself, *This is so Marti Scott. She is setting up relationships in the places of division. She makes connections in the intersections of alienation. She cannot, she will not let marginalization and isolation be.* I have known of Scott's work for thirty years: her creativity, her commitment to the poor, her capacity to assess and then enable the skills and capacities of a community, her work in organizing and building the power of a people. And all of these are based in an unshakable conviction that we are all co-creators with God. She is a practitioner of "alchemy"; she takes stop signs, garbage, gardens, free refrigerators, and homiletical forays into *The Wizard of Oz,* and they miraculously become justice ministry and fun!

Doing Change with and through the Denomination

Action in and through a denomination is usually a form of macro or at least *meso* change. Erin Counihan, however, reported on the work of her church with the General Assembly of the Presbyterian Church (U.S.A.). She was called by J. Herbert Nelson, the Stated Clerk of her denomination, who wanted the upcoming Assembly in St. Louis to be different from those of the past. He wanted this meeting to have "a hands-on element" that would be bold and faithful. As Counihan talked with some of her colleagues in St. Louis, they were concerned that the denomination might come in and prescribe what needed to be done. So they asked Nelson to join them in community projects they were already doing. Counihan confesses that Nelson was someone she greatly admired, so she was hesitant to make such a suggestion. But he was quite open to the idea. This came on the heels of the killing in Ferguson, so the wider city was continuing to deal with that.

When the leaders of the denomination came in, they and the local people brainstormed possibilities. "We came up with an idea from down on the ground," she says. Local groups wanted to close the St. Louis medium security jail, called the City Workhouse, because of inhumane conditions at the facility, including the lack of air conditioning in St. Louis summers. Advocates for closure wanted to take budget savings from its closing to invest in other programs they believed would improve the community. So Counihan and other local people recommended that the Assembly take up a collection for the closing of the jail project and that they engage in a march down the street to protest of the facility and to turn the money over to the appropriate people.

The biggest issue that arose in the Assembly's considerations of the action was that some members wanted to get a permit for the march. The local people were unwilling to pursue a permit, insisting, "We don't get permits in St. Louis." They explained to the Assembly leadership, "The streets belong to us." And so, the Assembly leadership supported the march without a permit. Hundreds of people participated. Counihan added, "There was no way the city of St. Louis would arrest all of those White people." There were local activists present, and an Assembly offering of fifty-three thousand dollars was made to this local effort. This contributed to the closing of the Workhouse in June 2021 by Mayor Tishaura O. Jones, fulfilling one of her campaign promises.

Counihan appreciated the fact that this was a collaborative effort between the General Assembly and St. Louis locals. "We got local support because we did it the local way, and we got Assembly support because we took initiative with the denominational leadership." She proclaimed that this experience with the General Assembly was a powerful learning experience for her: "Sometimes I forget to dream or think as big as I need to." She then underlined the fact that the General Assembly now does this kind of action in every host city.

Singing, Silence, and Green Tomatoes

I don't want to end this chapter on doing change with micro actions that factor into macro events. To be sure, these are very important, but I want to learn, again and again, the significance of the small things these pastors do. For that reason, I turn to the interview with Nancy Dennis and her work with singing, silence, and green tomatoes. Her congregation of about thirty people consists of two adults in their thirties, seven youth ages six through sixteen, and the rest are ages fifty to seventy. All are working-class people. "We don't always see things the same way," she says. "We may not be liberal on all issues, but we acknowledge things as we see them."

When approaching a new venture, she seeks to find someone in the congregation who has "experience, skill, knowledge, and capacity" to provide leadership and take on the work. They have local church meetings every month to find out where people are, what's on their minds, and what seems to affect them. They encourage each person to be a brother or sister to members of the congregation and to their neighbors.

The church is located near an antebellum plantation in Unionville, Maryland. This village on the outskirts of Easton was settled by ex-slaves and Black soldiers who came back from the Civil War. Land for the church and school was donated by sympathetic Quakers. The former Union soldiers purchased land from the Quakers to build homes near the church. Over time, the small community evolved in the general area of the former plantation. St. Stephen's church cemetery is one of three sites in Maryland added to the Underground Railroad Network.

Dennis says that there are racial tensions in the community that have recently gotten ugly. A few White people in trucks started driving through Black neighborhoods making noise and being threatening. In other incidents, Black educators reported White parents making derogatory comments at school and directly to them. But she also acknowledged that White people did help with an ancient tree that had fallen in the church's cemetery after a bad storm, and that a new pastor from a nearby White church was working with them to foster better relations. So she insisted that one "must not paint with a broad brush," and that, "While hard 'Trumpers' make most of the noise, they don't represent the majority." Still, she says too many White people support the former president's actions for fear of losing privileges—even if it is at the expense of their humanity and their professed faith in Christ.

In response to this tension, another local church began a reading project akin to a book club, and a few other churches joined in. The idea was to read a chapter a week about race and then to talk about each person's own experience. Dennis indicates that they found a real difference of culture in this activity. They struggled with the issue of "those who don't think the way we do. Some Whites did not want to come because they felt they were being blamed for social inequalities." Dennis insisted that her church's people wanted "to talk about the different ways we see things, not to blame." But this was not working. Although a small working group met faithfully to read and navigate through issues, they continued to look for other ways to engage more people.

They came up with the idea of each church selecting hymns from their respective hymnals, that is, from those of the AME and the Episcopal Church. When they came together to sing, the Spirit of the Lord moved among them. This time of singing worked so well that some thought it should be recorded, but others did not want other people to see what they were doing. The group pledged confidentiality, and it opened things up and led to "good, honest conversations."

Dennis spent a good portion of our interview talking about silence, insisting on its importance not only diagnostically but prescriptively. People become silent at different times and for different reasons, and each occasion means something. For example, she does her shopping in Kent County. At one store, where she shops, she finds herself ignored. One of those who ignored her was a computer technician who had been in her office, but he would not acknowledge her presence at the seafood counter. At the same time, she reports other occasions when people greet her, and everything is fine. "It's a mixed bag," she states.

The question for her is what to do with silence. She has developed a bit of an agenda. First, she looks for people who know her and trust her and will tell her what others won't say. She acknowledges that there is a difference in the perspectives of city and rural people, and that there are stereotypes on each side. She believes also that her gender is sometimes as big of a factor as her race. But it is a struggle each time because the silence means something different on each occasion and with different people.

At the same time, people say she's different, and she certainly has found different ways to connect with others. For instance, when she goes to the store, she specifically orders green tomatoes. This initially wasn't an intentional tactic of hers, but she discovered that when she says she just wants green tomatoes, people will laugh. This begins a connection, perhaps even a relationship. She also found that people like her pound cakes, and that this opens doors. She drops sympathy cards when someone has lost a family member. Or, if someone is in an accident, she will call to see if they want her to drop by. If they do, she goes. If they are a member of another church, she will call the pastor and ask if they mind if she goes to the hospital.

Having been pastor at the church now for twelve years, she stated that she relies on her lay members for many things, believing that "If you take care of them, God will send you a core group to work with.

You take care of people, and some people will reach out and take care of you."

I was impressed that Dennis had a host of smaller practices that she had learned and used effectively—yes, as a coach; yes, as a pastor; yes, as a Black woman; and, yes, through a range of events, of being ignored, of being excluded, and of just being unacknowledged. I thought to myself, what a school of learning all that must be. Perhaps it's only there that you learn these things about singing, silence, green tomatoes, and anticipate hugging again.

Doing Change in a Small Town

Jeremy Troxler said that micro practices are not always done consciously and are hard to identify, a response that indicates he already has critical awareness of the topic. In terms of justice ministry, he was able to report his past work in a church in a small town in Spruce Pine, North Carolina, an Appalachian community of about twenty-five hundred people. Because this ministry was now a couple of years behind him, he was able to look back on a special case of justice work with appropriate distance. Remembering back to the 2016 election, immigration had become a hot topic. Years prior, Ethan Allen had closed their Spruce Pine furniture factor. Several mining companies had also closed, making times hard for many people in that community. Located in a very conservative area, Trump votes came in 7-to-1.

One day, Troxler received an email from a man who wanted to talk with him. Reportedly, the email went out to more than twenty clergy, but Troxler was the only one to respond. So, they talked. The man divulged that he was an atheist, somewhat of a lefty, and he wanted to submit a proposal advocating for the rights of local immigrants to go to the city council and to the county. He wanted clergy and local churches to help. Troxler agreed to reach out to some ministers, but he was also clear that the clergy and the man with the proposal needed to talk to the immigrant community first. Their voices were to be privileged.

Troxler also believes that groups of this kind need to begin with the question, "How are you feeling now?" This often leads to an outpouring of pain and to stories of hard trouble. The stories told move and touch people and motivate them to build an alternative community, suggesting that the sharing of pain and trouble are only half the work, and that decision and action to make change and to build a different community are the next part of the work. The work only begins with the articulation of hurt and struggle but finds completion as a community in the decision to organize and take on the sources and the powers of captivity.

Following up, spreading the word, and recruiting partners from the neighboring School of Crafts, their first meeting drew fifty people. Calling themselves *Vecinos*, which in Spanish means "neighbors," the group began to organize. They agreed to focus on four areas of support: sanctuary, advocacy, legal, and transportation, or S-A-L-T. They formed four small working groups in each area, beginning with offering legal assistance.

Troxler says he learned "two little things." First, that they needed to ask the Hispanic people to speak first. Sometimes they had to tell the White people to be quiet so that there was space for other people to talk. Second, that Anglos often wanted to move directly to solutions, while Latinos wanted first "to neighbor."

He then turned to what it meant to *be* with another. It required five things. The first is to be physically present, face to face and in the same space. Second, give attention to and concentration on each other. Third, accept the mystery of each person—one who is not to be controlled, manipulated, and who is always more complex than we think them to be. Fourth, participation and partnership are required in which no one dominates and everyone both gives and receives. And finally, the fifth is that it is essential to avoid using one another instrumentally. We must see all people as intrinsic ends in themselves.[29]

One practice used to good effect was sitting in a circle in silence and taking notes. This practice helped to center the group and encourage listening, and, he says, "It helped us to know what we were going to follow up on." Troxler felt that this exercise helped to form real relationships and the building of trust. "As trust was built, beautiful things happened, all little things," said Troxler. "People began to ask about how to embody, to institute what we were about." Church people began to interact more with Hispanic/Latino kids in the community. Some in his church began to think about what could be done, for example, through an after-school program. They went to local schools to ask what was needed, by which age group, and on what day. "But," Troxler hastened to say, "we always asked the people most impacted by it first."

The church received a grant from the Duke Endowment and began a new reading program in the afternoon, hiring people to teach. Volunteers from the church read with Latino children, especially with kids who had no family members to help them. They got spots on the town's radio station and articles in the local newspaper. Summing up all that had happened, Troxler said, "All of these things were small steps, and their accumulation led to this program. Prior to this time, for example, there were no other afternoon school programs in our community. It was the little actions, the face-to-face relationships, which built this work."

He did mention one other thing that he called a bit of a miracle: a couple in the church unexpectedly won the lottery. They quietly gave 10 percent to the church, leading Troxler to say, "I'm going to take the Devil's money." It aided a lot of people, including the after-school program for children.

I asked Troxler about his conviction concerning the importance of the rural church. He told me that in college he received a prestigious scholarship to study medicine, but his deepening relationship with Jesus (and "especially the Jesus of Philippians 2") led him in a different direction. He remembered Henri Nouwen, who left Harvard Divinity School to care for a man with developmental disabilities, and Troxler confided, "God got a hold of me." Troxler wanted his life to be something different, to go in a different direction. He was enchanted by those who turn away from the "world's success" to "the real kingdom of God stuff among the least." That captivated him; it grabbed him. "Climbing to the bottom of the heap, I believe that's where Jesus can best be met and where we are shaped. To the degree that I have done that, my life is better."

He is in a big church now, but he said, "Those years in a small church were the best years of my life, and I was being used by God there more than anywhere else." Troxler understood that a wonderful life could be lived in a rural community and that "you can make a generational difference in a small church."

Rural people stay, he continued, "They are not moving. I'm struck by the goodness of that because so much of ministry is relational, and sustained relationships over a long time in a community create opportunities for God to do things that are truly special."

In keeping with this attitude toward others, when I asked him how he deals with the assholes, his answer was so beautiful that I quote it in its entirety:

"I try my damnedest to love them. I see that part of their personality as their brokenness, their sinfulness. I refuse to see them as evil; the image of God is there. In fact, the world may need assholes. We develop courage from them, patience, character, and long-suffering. Assholes are an anvil where you hammer out love. Not only that, but you also learn more from assholes than from people who are easy to love. God can use them for our sanctification. And sometimes, assholes can put me to shame by their generosity. One asshole in my church really is way more generous than I will ever be. He cooks meals for funerals."

Troxler's ministry took place in a small conservative town with an overwhelming majority of Trump voters. Yet amazing things happen when you get real people in friendly proximity with others so that their humanity shows through. Getting in circles, the practice of silence, following up, and building trust, these things can run past ideology and open doors closed by the distance of privilege and complacency of "the way we've always done it." Bringing together strange mixes of churches, atheists, sheriffs, schools, a large foundation, lifelong local people, Spanish-speaking immigrants, angular personalities, kids, and even a couple who won the lottery can be a kind of Pentecostal event, not occurring in just one moment and place but formed in gatherings of the Spirit where strangers who speak different languages suddenly understand each other. Community is formed, and new life begins.

A Small Urban Congregation Becomes a Seven-Day-a-Week Church

"If we are to work in the community, most of our prophecy is to the people of God, only some to kings and rulers." Traci Blackmon understands this and is committed to working with people of other faiths, an important ingredient in her previous ministry in Ferguson, Missouri. At the same time, she is clear that we are called to be true disciples if we are to follow Jesus. Blackmon says, "This means we go to work with both the Bible and with service, bread, and drink. We need to have food and diapers. Yes, with the Bible in one hand, but with resources in the other. Jesus both preached and fed people."

She continues, "We did voter registration work, and we did it the same way. We do what we do because we are compelled by the gospel." For example, in the mobilization of voters in Ferguson, they took eighteen hundred people to the polls. When asked how they accomplished such a feat, she explained it was by covenanting, by organizing churches, and by getting out their own volunteers and physically taking people to the polls. Even more, she said, "We did not use grant monies; we paid our own way."

She made another perhaps unexpected point, "If we are doing the work out of discipleship and call, we work with people who 'vote wrong' in my opinion, who stand in 'the wrong place.'" She explained, "Prophetic ministry is doing what God wants you to do."

Blackmon then transitioned to a discussion of the church she pastored in Ferguson, a small congregation with a large sanctuary and about twenty-five members. Only about a dozen of those attended church. "These folks were bruised. Their hopes were shattered; they had moved out of the neighborhood; and they only came back to serve the church."

One Sunday, Blackmon lead them in a conversation about the church, but the stories they told about its life and the community were no longer true. The neighborhood had changed. People no longer owned their houses in the neighborhood; they were renters. The community itself had become a location of pawn shops, liquor stores, and fast food restaurants. In the local school, 85 percent of the children received free lunches.

Following this, she preached a sermon entitled "The Door of the Church Is Open." In that message, she said, "Jesus is the door, and our door should be open." She asked the congregation if the church would be different if the doors were opened. She asked what would happen if people came in who did not look like them, who could not pay the electric bill, the water bill, and the other expenses of the church. She then said, "I am not the church, you are. If you want to be the church, we have to open the doors to people who don't look like us."

They began opening the building at no charge to groups in need of space. They invited in community organizations and others who learned to incubate in that space. And in the process, they became a seven-day-a-week church. The neighborhood endured so much violence that they began hosting funerals free of charge. The year before Michael Brown was murdered, a young woman was killed in the neighborhood in a drive-by shooting. Blackmon presided over her funeral, and the young woman's best friend came. Like her deceased friend, she was twenty-three years old, but she had not been part of the church. On the way out of the funeral service she asked for Blackmon's phone number, which Blackmon provided. But Blackmon did not hear from her until the day Michael Brown was killed. That day, the young woman and her children had walked up on Brown's body, still lying where he had been shot. She called Blackmon and told her that Blackmon had been her pastor since that time a year earlier, and that she needed the church.

Blackmon then said, "The most important thing we can do is to remember our call to be priestly and prophetic." She meant not merely as an institution, but as a gathering of people, a community that understands what God is asking of us. Reflecting something of her own struggle, she told me that every day she has to decide whether she is going "to love or to hold out for hate." She seeks to hear the Spirit's teaching, and she wishes she could get it right. Her call is to follow as a disciple and to see people as Jesus does. She claimed that "when we work for justice, we meet people who hold us accountable." This is one place from which she draws strength. She then added, "You've heard it said, but I say to you, not an eye for an eye . . . but helping people reconcile with the divine and with other people."

Blackmon concluded our interview observing, "We are in a unique place right now. We don't have clear answers; we have to deal with things that are antithetical to the gospel—the chasms have come. It's a very difficult time. We use definitions to place ourselves in opposition to each other." She spoke about Phyllis Tickle's thesis that every five hundred years the church goes through a renewal process. Perhaps we are in that time, Blackmon wonders. "I'm not afraid of the church dying. We've got problems, but we are not going to die. We are being reshaped and reformed." She interrupts this line of thought: "There is not left or right, but only the gospel. We have the same gospel now." The question is, "How can we sit down and reconcile with each other? Our dogma will hold, but how we treat each other is crucial on both sides."

I confess that a baseball analogy came to my mind when she told me that her church in Ferguson had about a dozen attendees and a total membership of twenty-five. I thought to myself, *That's like being behind ten to nothing in the bottom of the ninth. How in the world do you turn that around?* The answer, in Blackmon's case, is a host of small practices that snowball into major change: being prophetic and priestly, following Jesus by providing food and diapers, covenanting with churches, using volunteers, opening the doors of the church, being a space for community organizations, and offering the building for funerals free of charge. All of these speak of a profound faith conviction and of a confidence in the church. My baseball analogy failed. Scoring eleven runs in the bottom of the ninth is not an adequate description of what happened in Ferguson. It was more like a resurrection.

Behind the Scenes in a Context of Sweltering Oppression

Edwin King Jr. is the bravest White man I know. We were students at both Millsaps College and the Boston University School of Theology in the late fifties and early sixties. He went back to Mississippi as the chaplain at Tougaloo College, a private, historically Black college in Jackson associated with the Church of Christ. In that position, he was a key White ally during the civil rights movement. Arrested, beaten, ostracized, castigated by the local press and even the national media on occasion, and very nearly losing his life in a suspicious auto accident, King is described as "the most visible White activist in the Mississippi movement" by historian John Dittmer.[30] In my interview with King, I was especially interested in the micro practices he used under those highly oppressive circumstances.

He says, "The key thing is to let people know they are not alone. You have to encourage people; you have to let them know that they can get through it." Sometimes, King said, "It's almost a fake optimism, but there were people who thought they were absolutely alone." Such isolation had to be countered.

He then said, almost talking to himself, "Most of the time God is on our side and suffering makes me better. It helps the community go on." With that he went into a very helpful commentary about small meetings and how important they were during the mid-sixties and after in Mississippi. He spoke of the need "just to be able to manage to be together for a few months," and that "The important thing is to convince grass roots people to believe in themselves."

In those years, King wanted people in the church to start moving. He had reliable connections with good people. He also knew that they would have sharp conflict over the issue of race with others. He was convinced that there were also good people of status like William B. Selah, pastor of Galloway UMC, the prestigious Methodist Church in Jackson, and with Roy Clark, pastor of another significant congregation, who would later be elected bishop and serve in Tennessee. He knew they were good on the issue of race. He also knew that they were in highly polarized and volatile congregations. Many others were in similar circumstances, and "many of these people did not believe that anything they could say or do would work."

King decided that he would focus on institutions, and he chose Millsaps College and the church. He understood that change—via demonstrations, confrontations, boycotts, etc.—would have to come from within the Black community. The White community needed to believe there were things they could do. So along with other civil rights activists, King started doing church visits and voter registration behind the scenes. They also held concerts, and White Millsaps students would buy tickets they then gave to friends who were Black. King said, "We did little things just to get people in integrated settings." They also encouraged people of mixed races to sit together in venues that would welcome them and not have people walk out the door in protest. They also tried to attend segregated public events. These micro practices consisted of opening the door to art or music or other social events that could be "above the cultural/racial conflict." They sent a Black Tougaloo student with a White British student to a concert at which they were both arrested, but the report in *The New York Times* was a gain for the movement.

King states that he oversaw strategizing, but not conducting the actions himself. Rather, he was working with Millsaps students and faculty and especially with Carol Bergmark, the wife of Robert Bergmark, professor of philosophy at Millsaps College. He also worked with women from the church who felt they were not doing anything important. But King countered that claim, as he believed that all those small meetings with a diverse group of people (read: not White men) prepared the way for the future by often attending interracial gatherings.

Getting people in these meetings truly contributed to the cause. He remembers that before the 1963 March on Washington that Medgar Evers, a great civil rights leader in Mississippi who was later assassinated, and Martin Luther King Jr. encouraged these kinds of church meetings and agreed to cooperate with them. Also, behind the scenes were meetings with pastors Selah and Clark who, for example, asked that racially integrated teams not be sent on Easter because they thought they could have the churches open by the summer to interracial worship and meetings. This kind of collaboration was going on constantly underneath the surface.

There were also secret meetings of other clergy, Black and White together. At one time, Selah, under heavy pressure, got three White men from his church to meet clandestinely with Black civil rights workers. A good deal of this began with interracial communications between lesser-known people instead of the notable names one would assume. King describes it as a "let's talk about it" setting. He said at one point in the interview that their job was "getting people to believe there were small things they could do." People were making church visits or, where it was possible, registering voters. "We were doing little things to get people in integrated settings."

What came through to me in King's comments was the building of a network of relationships as an alternative to the violently dominated circumstances under which they lived. This network was building connections. It was the setting in place of a new time, a new reality. Not a perfect world—I suspect King knew that as well as anyone—but certainly even in its imperfection, a world moving in new directions beyond "a night already devoid of stars" as Martin Luther King Jr. had named it. I often think of the church as an alternative community; in these cases, it was an alternative network, the building of a covert community now for another time and place in the future.

I remember in the mid-sixties that Peggy and I drove to Tougaloo College to visit King and his wife, Jeannette, another fellow Millsaps and Boston University alum who had been arrested in Jackson while participating in a protest demonstration led by Medgar Evers in 1963. Peggy and I were visiting in their campus housing living room, sitting on the couch with our backs to the large window on the street-side of the place. As we got into the conversation, King responded to my question about the threats and intimidations of living in the South and being active in the civil rights movement there. I asked how he and Jeannette were able to do it. He admitted that it was difficult, that the Ku Klux Klan had recently driven onto the Tougaloo campus and fired shots into the houses there. At that point in the conversation, I felt myself performing a slow slide—I wanted it to be unnoticeable—down into a lower position on the couch, seeking to be beneath the window and out of the range of gun fire that I prayed would not be forthcoming. I remember saying to myself, "Ed and Jeannette live under this kind of threat all the time. How in the world can they do it?" I guess I'm saying that some of you who read these pages may not find these small group meetings as terribly important or requiring much courage or devotion. I urge you to give it a second thought, especially thinking in the context of the closed society of Mississippi in the sixties.

Throughout our conversation, the points I took from King's comments above were continually interlaced with stories about other things going on, many of them micro practices. He told a long narrative about working in the late sixties with Al Lowenstein, a one-time congressman and an important figure in the Democratic Party. These were occasions for developing local strategies that would also influence the Democratic Party nationally. They plotted to get the kind of national and international audiences that could support state and national civil rights while restraining the violence of racist government agencies, civic associations, and organizations in Mississippi and beyond.

King worked closely with Medgar Evers, Fannie Lou Hamer, Bob Moses, Martin Luther King Jr., Ernst Borinski, and others. As King and I talked, I was struck repeatedly by an entire range of micro settings in which strategy and tactics were designed and later implemented. Part of these led to the Woolworth's sit-in of 1963, the Mississippi Summer of 1964, the organization of the Mississippi Freedom Democratic Party, which challenged the national convention of the Democratic Party, and others. Indeed, it is quite clear that none of these larger efforts could've ever been considered, planned, or acted out in the Mississippi of that time without a host of micro practices. Indeed, in such times and places it is difficult to imagine the civil rights movement itself happening apart from such micro practices with their imagination, strategy, stealth, networking, coordination, and ventures.

You may wonder about the applicability of such clandestine, behind-the-scenes collaborations today, but I can think of several contemporary settings in the United States characterized by such deep polarization politically, economically, socially, and culturally that such face-to-face meetings can have very important roles to play. The necessity of such practices in some contexts continues today.

Having considered circumstances, however, where the state and the public square were dangerously oppressive, it seems appropriate to turn now to situations where the church is called to engage the public square directly, even invite them into the church itself to pursue the common good.

The Public Square and Convening Authority

Virtually from the beginning of our interview, Joel N. Martinez talked about "the public square." That language, that sphere of life, and that social arena have been a central part of his ministry as a pastor, an agency executive, and later a bishop. Because the study in this book is of clergy, my interview with Martinez focused on his pastoral ministry in Dallas, San Antonio, and El Paso, Texas. Most of his comments focused on the public square and how to bring that square and the larger community into interaction with the church, especially with key leaders of his congregations. His key concept was "the convening authority/power of the pastor" and its central role in the practice of doing justice ministry. These were not abstractions for him, and he immediately started telling stories out of his work as pastor in the three cities he served in three different decades, indicating something of the ongoing value of his claims about a pastor's convening authority.

In 1966 in Star County, Texas, farmworkers went on strike. Cesar Chavez sent in organizers to put in place a local unit and confront the local growers. When this action occurred, the Texas Rangers came down on them hard. The Roman Catholic Bishop Humberto Medeiros supported the workers and invited Chavez to speak in San Juan, Texas.[31] That June, Martinez went to hear Chavez and joined a gathering of the local farmworkers' unit and several other pastors. That began a long history of Martinez with the farmworkers' movement. Part of this work included the call for a long march to Austin to put pressure on the Texas legislature. Martinez reports that a young Catholic priest stood up at the meeting when this march was proposed and simply said, "If we begin this march, we must finish it and go all the way." They finished the march.

With these actions, Martinez's church became a depository of food and money for the farmworkers. They brought in Leo Nieto, an executive of the Texas Council of Churches to speak at his church. It was a packed house. Nieto laid out the challenges of racism, the struggles of farmworkers and their families, and the importance of these struggles to the people of Texas.

Martinez made the point that you must "get the congregation in touch with what is going on. This means you have to bring things into the local church." Talking about an issue is not enough; the agents of the public square must be engaged within the very walls of the local congregation. This is one of those places where the pastor's "convening power" is crucial. "We need pulpits that walk, not only those we preach from," he concluded.

I understand that bringing large numbers of people into a social gathering can be understood as a macro practice, or, at least, a *meso* practice, but the convening authority of the pastor occurs in a host of micro practices—meetings with individual leaders, sessions with small groups in the church, touching base by telephone or emails or text messaging, making pastoral calls, even visits with the sick and those homebound. The pastor's relationships in such a range of contacts provide the convening authority with its legitimating power and effectiveness.

Martinez's second story had to do with a public health issue, with the provision of clinics for the poorest people of the community. At that time, federal law required that every regional Council of Governments have a Health Planning Advisory Committee to review all federal health funding in their region. Martinez, while serving as a pastor in El Paso, was elected president of the Health Planning Committee of the West Texas Council of Governments (WTCG), which covered six counties. This council gave advice to communities establishing health centers, and these communities required the stamp of approval of the council, which had to okay all government contracts. The Texas Medical Association opposed this work of the WTCG. They did not want more clinics for the poor; instead, they were interested in providing the medical care instead and making the profit from it. The Council of Governments, however, argued that "we must invest in public health so that people don't have to come to hospitals." So Martinez invited these organizations to meet in his church. He says, "I wanted our people to come and hear what's going on. I wanted them involved in the dialogue."

Martinez told two other stories continuing to illustrate his point about the convening authority of the pastor. He explained, "It is not an advocacy, not a religious role as such, but rather to get people together for dialogue and conversation about things in the community, about the things on the front line." This involves practices like calling a city council member and inviting that person to the church to share what's going on. He further suggested that this will help your congregation better understand your preaching and writing. "It also makes it clear that you did not ignore the people of your church, that you respected them by inviting the public square into their presence in the congregation's building."

In his interview, Martinez emphasized meeting people where they are, especially in getting in touch with people who have high potential. "If you stay in a circle of the privileged, you are missing the opportunity to meet people you need to meet: the pushed out, the pushed down, and the pushed around." He stated that he has been in settings where "a real person gets up and just says it," meaning that they get what's going on in the community or around a given issue. Martinez then argued for cultivating that kind of person, suggesting that we need the wisdom to ask, "Who can shape and influence that kind of raw talent better than I can?" Martinez's point is that one must be alert to the talent that is available, and that clergy have a responsibility to recognize and develop that kind of talent. Making this point, he emphasized the talent of the mother of John and Charles Wesley. He claimed that "Susanna is the true founder of the Methodist movement, not John and Charles. She was the one who trained and formed those kids." Martinez's point here is not only about the importance of Susanna Wesley, but also the array of talent to be considered when speaking to the wide range of capacities we require in the work of justice.

Martinez named three other points in justice work. One is the telephone, a resource he has used for staying in contact with a wide variety of people in the church and in the larger community, even for holding people accountable. He told a story of a man who had begun skipping church, so Martinez called him to tell him, "Empty pews are the work of the devil." The man began attending again, and this same man "would later publicly testify that he got calls from me." Martinez also reported a comment from an acquaintance, "Joel, you must have a phone connected to your ear," and he admits that he was "always on the phone." While he did text and email, he used the phone to update others and to be updated, and Martinez was quick to say that he worked with the phone "not only to call and talk but to listen." He emphasized the importance of the phone as a listening device, especially in the work of justice.

Second, Martinez stressed the importance of working together, taking things step by step and not running past others who need to be included. His example here was the development of a health clinic, which necessitated cooperating with other churches and community groups, getting a grant, working personally with medical doctors, and doing things collaboratively with other key stakeholders. Later in the interview he spoke to the temptation of pastors to "take off on something, for it to become our thing." In opposition to such a tendency, he contends that "we need to hear from the public square."

The third grew out of an encounter with Ernesto Cortés Jr. at an Industrial Area Foundation organizing meeting. Cortés, one of the most famous community organizers in the United States in the last fifty years, did an extraordinary organizing job in San Antonio and was at the time the Executive Director of the West/Southwest Region of the IAF. Then a pastor, Martinez came late to the meeting being led by Cortés, and when he entered the room, Cortés asked, "Rev. Martinez, you are seven minutes late. Do you have something to say to the people here for disrespecting them?" Martinez learned from this confrontation the importance of being punctual and several other practices related to respect for people. Specifically, he spoke of being available, of not hiding behind an office door. He characterized Jesus as being radically available and cautioned, "Unless you are available, the people get the sense that you are too busy, too over-scheduled to pay attention to them." Being available instills the lesson that they are important.

Martinez recalled that the work of John Wesley was on the roadways, in the parks, and in the public square. He did evangelism, but he also did social work. The lesson for Martinez is that the future is being decided in public life. "We must show up in the marketplace, in the public square, and bring it into the life of the parish."

7

DISCIPLE LEADERSHIP

I have titled this chapter "Disciple Leadership" because the emphasis on leadership in the church today rumbles in my gut with problematic disturbances. I guess the primary reason is that we are called first to be followers, not leaders. I know that God does call out leaders like Moses, Rachel, David, Tamar, Jeremiah, Deborah, Jesus, the women at the tomb, Paul, Phoebe and many others we meet in scripture. But these leaders are spoken to by a sovereign God, and their principal role is to follow that divine leading.

But I have another problem. A good deal of the leadership material influencing our publications and thought comes from corporate America. If there is any group that has failed this country, it is corporate America. In the past forty years, the neoliberal corporate mentality that has dominated the economy and the political scene has emphasized deregulation of the economy, tax avoidance, anti-labor and union-busting policy, privatization, the off-shoring of jobs, hyperglobalization that has served wealth and riches to the detriment of the bottom half of the class structure. We have a plutocracy in the United States not seen since the Gilded Age. The most we can hope to learn from corporate leadership is what not to do.[32]

I am glad to say that as I talked with these clergy, I found versions of leadership rich in micro practices and quite at variance from that of corporate America. The difficulty is knowing where to begin, but I will start with credibility. As I do, I will grab snippets of wisdom from various of the clergy I interviewed along with more extended comments as appropriate.

Credibility

There is nothing more important in credibility than embodying one's commitment. I think here of Bill Breeden, whom we met earlier. He lived for a nearly two decades without electricity on less than six thousand dollars per year to avoid paying taxes to the US military budget. For five of those years, he and his wife, Glenda, lived in a teepee with their two children. Bill and Glenda have both been arrested for nonviolent disobedience. "Fortunately," he says, they only had to serve "short terms of incarceration."

Something of Breeden's prophetic fire and credibility was evident when his hometown of Odon, Indiana, named a street after another of its citizens, John Poindexter, who was President Ronald Reagan's National Security Advisor. The Reagan administration was deeply involved in the Iran-Contra affair at the time, and Breeden believed that the naming of a street after Poindexter was "a celebration of immoral behavior in the government." So, he not only stole the sign but held it for ransom for thirty million dollars, the amount of money that had been given to Iran for transfer to the Contras. Breeden was put on trial, convicted of a misdemeanor, placed in jail for a week and then on probation for two years. Howard Zinn reports that Bill Breeden was the only person to be imprisoned because of the Iran-Contra affair.[33] In addition, Breeden also made two trips from Bloomington, Indiana, to Posoltega, Nicaragua, delivering material aid, first during the Contra War in 1989 and again after Hurricane Mitch caused 11,374 fatalities in Central America in 1998. "The first trip included a four-day excursion in a Honduran military prison [as a prisoner!], all expenses paid, perhaps sponsored by the CIA," he said.

Arrested Credibility

John Flowers, whom we also met earlier, tells the story of the police coming into his church and arresting a homeless man and taking him across the street from the church to a hotel where they had a surveillance center. When Flowers heard this report, he took off immediately for the hotel, found the homeless man with the police, and stationed himself beside the former. When one of the officers asked who he was, Flowers identified himself and stated that he and the officer needed to talk. When the officer said that they would have to talk later, Flowers said, "You cannot just come into God's house and take this man away." The officer responded with a demand, "Sir, I told you to wait outside." Flowers countered, "Officer, no one has the right to come and take a man out of God's house!" The policeman then made the threat, "Sir, if you do not leave the premises now, I will place you under arrest."

Flowers did not want to be arrested, but he simply could not leave his "homeless brother down in that basement all alone with the security guard and those police officers." He told the police officer, "Go ahead and do what you have to do, but I will not leave my brother's side." With that he was handcuffed and taken outside on the sidewalk. There, a crowd of people from the church daycare center had assembled and witnessed the arrest of their pastor on behalf of one of their members. That one act cemented Flowers's credibility with the street people.[34]

Intrinsic Identity

We learned before from Stanley E. Basler the importance of establishing identity and credibility. He was able to work with both Democrats and Republicans, and reports that one Republican, who was Speaker of the House in Oklahoma when they first met, is now a key figure in Oklahoma and a co-collaborator with his prison ministry. There is a story behind the story here. Basler was invited by a lay leader of a local church to fill the pulpit on short notice for Labor Day weekend. Basler told him he would accept if the lay leader could ensure that the Speaker would be in attendance that Sunday. The lay leader did, and thus began the relationship of the Speaker to the prison ministry that continued even after he left the legislature.

This led me to wonder about the impact of the identity of these clergy on the people with whom they worked, but also on those who were opponents and, yes, even enemies. I realize that identity must first be an intrinsic value, something to which we hold because of the value it has in and of itself. It must not be reduced to an instrumental value—a means to some other extrinsic value—which then depletes its theological and moral substance. But I also think of the contagion of witness and, most important, the way that God can use our witness as vibrant testimony to what the divine is doing in the maze of human action and the dominations of history.

Why Identity

Traci Blackmon said that "the *why* matters" and is a key to identity. People do *why* from many different places. In her own case, she is deeply committed to her "yes to God and to Jesus" and sees herself as "an apprentice to them." For her, redemption is the goal. Recognizing that there is good and evil in all of us, she states that that's why she shows up in the streets and sometimes why she doesn't. Winning is not the goal, she says, but rather, "It is reconciliation and discipleship." It is "a pastoral mindset."

Blackmon goes on to say that the most important thing we do is be priestly and prophetic. She reports that when Michael Brown was killed in Ferguson, she knew that her work had to be scheduled around all that was going on in the street. She used a chart, she organized, she had a schedule, and she stood in the breach between police and youth. She pushed the question: "What's wrong here, what's needed here?" She maintains that to do this kind of ministry, one has "to create ownership" and give people "the opportunity to contribute and to voice their own views." She says, "You have to create ownership in a conscious way," and this "is an act of discipleship." She speaks further of her attempts to "move with the truth of scripture, not only because of scripture but also to be governed by scripture."

She finished this comment stating that one "has to be rooted theologically." In her view, the Bible is a collection of stories, and clergy must take the truth of those stories and translate it into the pain in the street. "What happens in the street may look like violence, but it is pain," and "we have to find that on both sides." Qualifying this last point, she states, "Sometimes, we also have to take a stand and call out what's going on." She then quoted Renita Weems: "The only difference between Peter and Judas is that Judas did not stick around for the benediction."

It is in this context that Blackmon understands identity. She gets that people come from unique and different places, and she sees activism as the acceptance of the mantle of discipleship, saying yes to Jesus. She's an apprentice for whom redemption is the goal and, I would add, a craft. Knowing there is good and evil in everyone gets her into the street and sometimes keeps her from going there. She is clear that the goal is not winning but rather discipleship and reconciliation, a pastoral mindset, a disposition to which she seeks to be faithful. She sees her identity as priest and prophet, which requires her to be between the police and the youth. Central to all of this is keeping and interpreting the biblical stories. Understanding herself in these ways leads to a hermeneutic of the street (my language) where who she is requires a re-interpretation of urban violence and pain. Yet sensitivity to pain leads her to take a stand in community arguments, conflicts, and violence. Even so, she wants us all to "stick around for the benediction."

Discipline

I was exhausted after my interview with Holly McKissick. Her discipline, her regimen of activity and work, the relationships she sustains, and the schedule she keeps are as challenging as those of anyone I met in the study.

She wants to be proactive and not reactive. So she takes attendance every week at church and triggers conversations with those present on Sunday morning. During the week she will look through the church directories for those she has not seen lately. She then texts or calls them.

She takes every person in the church to lunch on their birthday. Taking about an hour and a half for the meal and conversation, she loves to check in with people and attempts to always be there to share and to go deep in relationships. The day of our interview, McKissick had had lunch with a woman from her church before our meeting. She said, "I'm good at remembering people's lives and families and relationships." As she said this, I remembered that she had asked me about my wife, my two children, and one of my grandchildren by name as we began the interview. She also sends everyone in the church birthday and anniversary cards.

McKissick engages in regular practices, many of them daily. She runs five to six miles a day, journals, walks the dog, listens to podcasts, stays up to date on justice-related issues, and meets with several Protestant clergy and a local rabbi in a study group of the Torah portion of each Sunday's biblical lections. All of these things are in addition to her work in four broad-based organizing groups in the city.

At this point in the interview, she mentions the importance of showing up, going to meetings, acting, and being there ahead to help prepare. I can confirm this because I often see her at important meetings in the city. She embodies the adage, "Ninety percent of justice is showing up."

I asked how she stays at it. She said that she draws strength from the witness of those with whom she does the work of justice. In addition, she observed that "the people who are happy stay at it." She then connected "staying at it" to keeping a balance between activism and voluntarism. It is so important to get to know and work with the people who are poor. "If everybody would just take on one person, it would make a huge difference. There is a gift to this. Being engaged and forming relationships with the poor, is a gift. It is life-giving to be related to and work with the poor." She concluded, "Who you hang out with is very important." She added, "Very few of us Whites have been prosecuted. We have not gone to prison. I have never been persecuted for my faith." That is where she left it.

McKissick's discipline is populated with practices through which she attempts to be proactive. But note how relational the regimen is. Without these connections, she would not be able to sustain her level of work. She seems to be able to "metabolize" these relationships into the ongoing commitments and action of her ministry and life. Her own daily practices, the way she draws from the witness of others, her engagement in four organizing efforts in the city while participating as a volunteer with the poor all bespeak an embodiment of justice in micro practices that get translated into larger systemic work.

LGBTQ+, Beloved Community, and Humility

As a married gay man, David Meredith has struggled in The United Methodist Church. In the past, he was brought up on charges by his denomination. In the interview, he spoke of practices that have been significant on both issues of sexual identity and sexual orientation in his life. He turned first to spirituality and the necessity of a daily relationship with God through devotion, prayer, and Bible study.

Using the language of micro practices, he stressed how important it is to work at practices relating to God. Among these are theology, grace, and practicing the means of grace. He spoke specifically of "remembering my own belovedness, to live and ground myself in sacred space." He tells me that his micro practices of spirituality began when he was a seminary student at Saint Paul School of Theology, particularly in classes where theory and praxis were integrated.

He remembered being in community with other LGBTQ+ people in seminary and letting himself be exposed to the larger LGBTQ+ community. Without this, he says, "I could've become a closeted gay person, absent from myself and living in fear." He noted, "It takes courage to come out" and required holding on to his identity in a "community of beloved folks." The church he pastors is in Ohio, but he is also working with two trans people in justice ministry in Iowa, where their website focuses on worship, liturgy, and a liberated sexual orientation and identity. There is nothing better than "finding the shared passions, finding and nourishing community," he says.

I asked what he wished I had asked but did not. His answer was immediate. "The important question is, 'Who is at the center of justice work?'" He confesses, "I come into every situation with cultural arrogance. I need the control of humility. I need to center other voices. It is not about my cultural competence but about my cultural humility." He went on to say how important it is for people like him, as well as others of us by implication, "to center other voices. To work with someone else's gifts, to learn the wisdom of those who have suffered."

It is impressive how Meredith has integrated his life, his calling, and his work. A sustaining spirituality grounds him in a grace-centered life that enables him to remember who is central in his work and to form him in a cultural humility so that he can hear other voices.

Listening

Clergy are professional talkers. That is why it is vital that they to learn to listen. We turn again to Harold W. Garman because listening was so central to his bubble up theology and his approach to social change. In this section, I will focus on his work as founder of the Gaithersburg Beloved Community Initiative (GBCI). He and his wife, Jan, retired to Asbury Methodist Village in Gaithersburg, Maryland, in 2010. After settling there they heard a sermon, "The Cradle to Prison Pipeline," by Marian Wright Edelman at Foundry UMC in Washington, DC, on the commemoration of Martin Luther King Jr.'s birthday in 2011. Garman was motivated to get involved but was faced with the problem of living twenty-five miles away. Jan asked him, "Why don't you do something about the youth in Gaithersburg?" (Hearing the story in the interview, I was struck by the fact that the initiative for the GBCI began with Garman listening, a basic practice throughout his ministry.)

Beyond the fence of the 130-acre campus of Asbury on two sides were immigrant-dominated neighborhoods, and Gaithersburg has been characterized as one of the most diverse cities in the United States.[35] Garman wanted to see if he could get the people of Asbury involved with the youth in Gaithersburg. He began with conversations among the retirees at Gaithersburg, with the mayor of the city, a Black pastor who served as the Community Liaison for the County Executive, the Wesley Seminary Urban Ministry faculty, and others. They then hired seminary students to go into the community and listen to the stories of the people there. They asked three people recently released from the county penitentiary which age groups of children would be the most important to make an intervention with to prevent them from being incarcerated, and they were told fourth and fifth graders through high school. With this, the GBCI began meetings with high school youth and fourth and fifth grade teachers.

Listening to all these groups and others enabled the group to focus its efforts. They developed mentoring programs with middle schools in the area. For youth struggling with prejudice, racism, and exclusion in their schools and neighborhoods, they offered "Courageous Conversations" with persons who had lived through traumatic situations, including the Holocaust, racial integration in public schools, and internment camps for Japanese Americans. They had early literacy sessions for moms and toddlers and monthly meetings with Asbury residents to learn about the community outside the fence.[36]

Garman said, "The ideas just kept coming. It just happened, one thing after another." The result of all this listening was "the right idea at the right moment. It did not take much to get it going." GBCI had no full-time staff until about five years ago. At that point they had worked with close to one thousand neighborhood residents in eight programs. They have now trained and pay five immigrant mothers to lead the Early Steps program for moms and toddlers.

Further, they have access to community organizers; some are residents of Asbury, some are from a county-wide community organization (Action in Montgomery), and some are residents in the local community.

Through this process of expansive listening and the spontaneity of developing programs, Garman learned that two of the most important roles that GBCI could play were *collaborator* and *catalyst*. "The major collaboration we could offer was intergenerational since we had a good supply of seniors who were interested in working with children, youth, and adults from the neighborhood. And we learned that just because someone brings a good idea for a project, that doesn't mean GBCI has to do it; GBCI could encourage, share knowledge, and supply volunteers without taking responsibility for the operations."

I suspect the readers of a book like this will not allow Garman's humility to lead them to believe that he "just listened," as desperately important as that can be. But there is sophistication in what he reports. Note the great range of people *to whom* he listened. Recognize that he knew *what* to listen for and that he knew *how* to make connections among the people from whom he heard. And, more, think about how important it was to know how to take the next step, not only in the sequence of listening but in the order of pulling people together. As I listened to Garman, I realized that in a context such as his that micro practices cannot be just a smattering of exercises with no particular focus, direction, or procedural succession. There is a participative, indwelled capacity for knowing how to move even in a project of listening. Mere random conversations will not get at the domination, the exclusion, the marginalization, or the inequities of a setting like the one with which Garman engaged. Neither will it be part of the necessary directions for change. The point is that he listened, and he knew what he was doing.

Leadership in a Culturally Traditionalist Setting

As important as delegating is, as important as building a community is, as overwhelming as this work can be when one tries to go it alone, and as much as one needs both to give and to receive support, it is clear that discerning and enabling potential leadership is central to justice ministry. Mark Matheny pointed especially to the importance of recognizing, bringing out, and making use of emergent leadership in church and organizing work. Working in a setting where queer people were often excluded, his church organized a group of six singers called The Bridge. Three were Black and three were White. Three were straight and three were gay. They sang spirituals and blues, different genres of music from those of the choir. They had an annual concert and sang at other events in the church and in the city. Their themes were hope and freedom. Matheny says that everyone knew very well there were gay men in the group, but it was one of those "don't ask, don't tell" things.

During the interview, I remembered a conversation I had with my mother when I was young. Her best friend's brother was clearly gay, and everyone in my hometown of Brookhaven, Mississippi, knew it. I remember, like a videotape in my mind, Mama telling me that he was "different." That's as descriptive as she got. She told me that people "make fun of him and treat him bad." Then she added, "If you are ever there, and someone does him wrong, and you don't stand up for him . . . when you get home, I'm gonna whup your ass." I was two years younger than him and hardly able to intervene in such circumstances, which would usually involve people who were older than I and a whole lot stronger and better able to fight. I protested and implied that she was not sympathetic to him in every way—I knew she had questions about homosexuality—but my mother had an instant answer: "I don't even care if he's an SOB; he's our SOB."

I asked Matheny if something like that was at work with his group. "Absolutely," he responded. We briefly discussed the complexity of micro practices in which the "don't ask, don't tell" practice works on the one hand, and how it can be connected to the whole matter of relationships through family or local or friendship ties. Matheny reports that both factors were at work in bringing this singing group into a significant leadership role in his church and, to some degree, the larger community.

Please understand, I hate the fact that these kinds of practices continue to play out in communities that are otherwise so closed. At the same time, I can forget how easy it is to be critical when viewing from a distance the people who are working with the best they've got in a given time and place. When I find myself criticizing these practices because they are not enough, I remind myself that I am more typically in situations that are far more inclusive, and I am not challenged the way people are in circumstances that are more closed.

Further, let us not forget that Matheny was working to recognize and bring forth leadership in his congregation. This singers' group became important in musical leadership that involves both the congregation and the community. The subtleties and power of these kinships and relationships in the church and the community should not be missed, and their impact in the moment and in the long term should not be rejected.

Let me add one further note here. I have spent a considerable amount of my life studying, teaching, and writing about what Andrew Levison calls cultural traditionalist people.[37] I think of two practices of change that are central with such folk, the people with whom I was raised. The first is that change typically occurs by bringing the tradition forward. That is, make the case for change by means of something significant in the tradition and how it speaks to us and calls us to something new. Remembering particular people, calling forth situations from the past, reminding people of things we forgot, placing before us actions we need to remember—all these and more can serve to open the future.

Note also the practice of adding change to something traditional. Music that speaks of the biblical themes of faith, struggle, freedom, love and a better tomorrow was already important in Matheny's church. It was a small but monumental step to have The Bridge share that music and those themes with the church and the community.[38]

I am grateful to Matheny for the way he opens the complexity of the micro practices involved in discovering and discerning leadership, and also for the sophistication he manifests in working with the complexity of traditional forms of change.

Play and Rest

Work and witness require self-care and rest. So, I was glad to learn from Joseph Daniels Jr. how important these are in his life. "You can't do this work unless you do the personal disciplines that sustain it," was his opening comment on this topic of play and rest. "First, you have to have a prayer life, but you also need prayer partners," he emphasized. "You need people who will keep you accountable." He added, "You need people who keep you sanctified, who prevent you from being taken out of the game." He acknowledged that "it's easy to fall prey to temptation." A heavy workload can lead to loneliness, and loneliness can lead to succumbing to temptation. This is also where "you need to establish a community to stand with you, to uphold you, to be the church. These are things that help you stay healthy, so when the challenges come, you can stay faithful."

Moving next to the necessity of vacation, he said, "I like the beach, I like travel, I like to get away. Just chilling, being on the golf course, fishing, riding a bike." With Daniels, I was struck repeatedly by the load of work not only placed upon him but that he took upon himself. I felt relieved when he shared the variety of ways he takes time away and finds an alternative of micro practices to take care of himself in a committed life.

Take Care of Ourselves and Play

We met Billy Vaughan previously in the chapter on spirituality. As we talked, he emphasized that we need to take care of ourselves. We are physical beings, he said. And this needs to be taken seriously, to be honored. We must hold ourselves to self-care. This involves honoring the gift of physicality, not just our flesh and bones but our entire bodies, and holistically taking care of ourselves. Vaughn knows that self-care can be selfish, but we need to see the body as God-given and hold each other responsible for this gift.

Play is very important to Vaughan. When his children were young, he would come home from church, walk in to meet his children, and get down on the ground to play with them. First, he said, it kept him from taking himself too seriously. Second, "If those kids were going to take on deep values and take seriously their own narrative, they needed to play, but it was a mutual benefit between them and me." Now his youngest kid is thirty. They are close and doing well. "We are on a family Zoom every week."

He tells me that his children attended an interracial school where they were in the minority. "Because of our life in a multiracial church and the diverse neighborhoods in which we lived, they did not feel out of place. To the contrary, this diversity deeply enriched and shaped all our lives. It wasn't about ideology. This is who we were as a family; it's how we lived."

There is great wisdom in Daniels's and Vaughan's notions of self-care. I suspect all of us have seen how neglecting rest and play results in poor health, burnout, destructive affairs, and even death. Many people in justice ministry have fallen because they did not have creative leisure. Further, it may well be that the micro practices of relating to our families are the most important things we can do, not only to love them in Christ but to contribute to their own futures as healthy and whole persons.

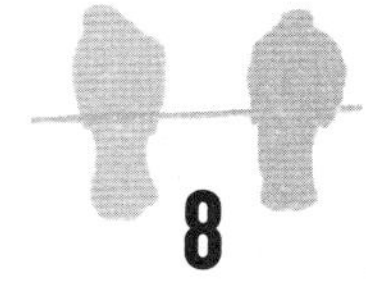

8

NONVIOLENCE

Practicing Nonviolence

Kristen Stoneking has made nonviolence central to her ministry and the framework by which she does administration and leadership. She indicates that there are no set principles of nonviolence, and she reports that she has learned much from people like James Lawson, who was a civil rights leader and an expert in nonviolence strategy and tactics, and the Pace e Bene Nonviolence Service, an independent, nondenominational organization that works to mainstream peacemaking that will empower people from all walks of life to prayerfully and relentlessly engage in nonviolent efforts for the well-being of all.[39]

Stoneking does however have her own list of principles/practices, which she outlines as follows:

- The humanity of all persons must be respected.

- Just means lead to just ends.
- We all have a piece of the truth and the untruth.
- Healing requires creativity.
- Power arises out of right relationship.
- Violence is rejected as a means to control and resolve disputes based on the belief that violence begets violence.
- We are not reducible to the evil we commit.
- Feelings, experiences, cultures and beliefs must be considered.
- An "us versus them" mentality is a distortion of reality.
- Nonviolence means an active commitment to peace and social justice.
- In nonviolence, actions are based in love.
- There is a willingness to accept suffering in order to create change.[40]

These principles are the foundation of her micro actions as a Christian. In her work she attempts to escape the historical dominance of Christianity "to re-orient into practices and relationships characterized by nonviolence and peace."

When Stoneking was newly ordained, she spent three years at a church in Lawrence, Kansas. But when she went to ministry in higher education in California, she found that church language was "less than useless." She had to code switch from speaking as a person from a dominant tradition to the language of those with whom she worked. For example, when she used the word "justice" on campus, it communicated judgment. It was a word that had no value in that context. Further, in that secular, West Coast setting, people were suspicious of the Cal Aggie Christian Association for whom she worked. She believed, however, that the people she met "wanted to make meaning and to be good persons." So they had lots of meetings and gatherings with different groups of people of faith and of no faith around the community. They attempted to listen to each other, and she avoided typical church language. For instance, a barrier to communication would be anyone who seemed to have an agenda to convert someone else so that they would not have a voice. Thus, Stoneking had a challenge: how to maintain Christian integrity on the one hand and honor different languages and agendas on the other. How does one communicate the life-giving character of Christianity and still be open to the life-giving dimensions of someone else's point of view or faith commitment?

These were the circumstances where she found nonviolence utterly essential. She would remind herself that we all have pieces of the truth, but also there are traces of truths we cannot see. To be sure, she believes that God revealed God's self, God's character, in Jesus Christ. For Stoneking the Christian path is essential to her life. "It is," she says, "the air I breathe." She would also then ask herself if her faith was exclusive or dominating? She came to believe that the Spirit of life is revealed in other traditions and that there is goodness and hope in those.

At this point in the interview, she returned to the practice of breathing together, which she described as the bedrock of her spirituality. She used an example from her campus ministry at the University of California, Davis when the police pepper sprayed Occupy movement demonstrators because of their refusal to remove their tents from the campus. In response, students surrounded the Surge II building on campus, where the chancellor was inside responding to the media regarding the incident. An assistant chancellor called Stoneking to come and mediate. Stoneking was aligned with Occupy, knew some of the students, and understood that they were trying to do something right. During the occupation of the quad, Stoneking's organization shuttled food to the student occupiers. Previously, she had engaged with many of the same students around Palestinian rights but also in opposition to antisemitism.

When Stoneking arrived at the Surge II building, she could feel the tension. She and a student named Tom Zolot, who was a Unitarian and an Occupy leader, were able to enter the building for a meeting with the chancellor. In this volatile context she knew that the relationships that had been built over time needed to be drawn on and called forth, and the breathing practice would connect with that. People needed to get in touch with their breath because it slows the heart and de-escalates tension.

Stoneking and Zolot told the chancellor that the students were holding the chancellor responsible for the harm that had occurred.[41] At the same time, they promised that the demonstrators would be nonviolent. After gaining concessions, Stoneking walked the chancellor out of the building and passed peaceful, seated students who had moved to one side of the walkway for them to pass. That the situation was tense and at least potentially explosive is suggested by the fact that one hundred thousand signatures were later gathered online asking for the chancellor's resignation.

Stoneking told of another event in which she engaged in nonviolent action at the Special Session of The General Conference of The United Methodist Church in 2019, the world meeting of her denomination. The action occurred after what Stoneking called "a violent vote" by the majority of delegates to continue what was then the official position of the denomination that "the practice of homosexuality is incompatible with Christian teaching" and, further, that "self-avowed practicing homosexuals" cannot be ordained in the denomination. This also confirmed the position that UMC pastors were not authorized to perform marriages between LGBTQ+ people.

With that, those who had hoped for policy change began singing in anger, sadness, mourning, and protest. Then, however, those who had voted for continuing the traditional policy began singing themselves. Stoneking wrote later, "For a moment, like two opposing pep bands in a college basketball game, the voices drowned each other out. It was an image of a deeply broken body."

Stoneking and her colleague Brian Adkins decided to go to the floor of the conference to pray during an open session. They walked behind the stage at the front of the meeting, past security guards, and onto the floor, well in sight of delegates there and spectators in the balcony. Once seated, Stoneking engaged in Tonglen meditation, a Buddhist practice in which one breathes in suffering and breathes out peace that she had learned from the work of Vietnamese monk and peace activist Thich Nhat Hanh. It felt like all she could offer.

In the interview, Stoneking said that her primary approach to making decisions is through consensus, believing that voting is problematic because it entails winners and losers. Consensus, on the other hand, allows for options. She understands that sometimes decisions are required, but a consensus approach provides a way to see and to hear everyone. She said that the way we make small decisions affects how we make big decisions, and that our methods of decision making are a key to nonviolence.

She then turned to the matter of restorative justice. Rooted in a kin-dom reality, this is countercultural because it respects humanity. She often reminds herself that no person is reducible to the evil they commit, and that some people are not conscious of their words when they say the wrong things. From a Christian perspective, we all need forgiveness because we are all fundamentally broken. The problem is that we don't always see ourselves as broken.

Stoneking is convinced that healing requires creativity. She believes that Christianity is life-giving, but she admits that Christianity has a dimension of domination. And sadly, this is true in a time when we, as a people in the United States, are not good at working with complexity in our issues. All these things make the commitment to nonviolence essential. It is a major set of practices by which "we can eclipse the ways rigidity can do harm."

Micro Practices of Nonviolence

JustFaith Ministries is a nonprofit based in Louisville, Kentucky, that creates and employs small group programs with the goal of advancing "peace, racial equity, and a sustainable world."[42] Because of her success implementing JustFaith programs in the local church, Deborah Weatherspoon has become co-chair of its national board of directors,

The process at JustFaith can be applied to many different social issues—such as gun violence—but the basics are the same. Weatherspoon explains, "Through small group programs we help people deepen their faith, invite learning, and inspire action around contemporary social issues. Participants leave our programs better prepared to do justice in their local communities and beyond. In JustFaith, people go through a facilitation process and from that learn to do intervention on an issue." The process works from basic micro practices all the way up to lobbying on legislation.

The programs include questions and spiritual practices to help participants discern their next steps in acting on behalf of justice. Each session of a program includes prayer and a covenant to be in a small group and meet once a week, and each program in the series is composed of eight-week sessions. They also study scripture and engage in events outside the group through a process of immersion. In all of this, participants are asked to discern where God is calling them.

Weatherspoon served a predominantly White, middle-class, well-funded United Methodist church as an associate pastor when she first learned of JustFaith Ministries programs. She introduced JustFaith into their small group process, and one of the outcomes was that the congregation created a nonprofit organization for feeding others. Nationally, JustFaith graduates are behind the creation of multiple nonprofits and are often the volunteers supporting existing organizations such as Catholic Charities. Other efforts in the area are working on issues like immigration.

Weatherspoon co-facilitated JustFaith's program on civil dialogue with Kristin Stoneking, whom we just met. Incorporating non-violent communication, she says, "The group discusses the way we use language and seeks to encourage vulnerability in conversation." The program uses video resources in small groups to focus and practice nonviolent interaction. JustFaith provides facilitator training and support so that at the end of this program, each participant is prepared to facilitate another group in their ongoing work.

I find the history of JustFaith Ministries inspiring. Their national partners include organizations like Bread for the World,[43] whose mission they support by having participants write letters to legislators on the farm bill, give testimony about the issue in churches, and bring the letters to the worship service to be blessed before they are sent to legislative representatives. This is Bread for the World's Offering of Letters program, supported by JustFaith small groups in local churches.

Weatherspoon is passionate about JustFaith, having been on its board of directors since 2017. The organization has primarily based its programming in congregations, but it is now moving into small groups in the neighborhoods of congregations. They are also exploring relationships with multi-faith organizations, where they create programs described as "spiritual" instead of solely Christian. In her own case, Weatherspoon got involved in JustFaith's work on preventing gun violence and was asked to be a faith leader by the Oakland chapter of Moms Demand Action for Gun Sense in America.[44]

JustFaith is pervasively characterized by micro practices that involve learning—for example, using videos and the study of scripture—but also training in the use of nonviolent language and peaceable participation in a small group. It engages in spiritual practices in structured covenantal settings, yet it also immerses people in community walks and other actions. As Weatherspoon says, these range "from basic micro practices all the way up to lobbying on legislation." I think, too, of the kind of bonding that can occur in settings like these, especially as they are embraced in prayer, immersed in action on an issue, and encouraged to discern God's calling. This is both formation and transformation.

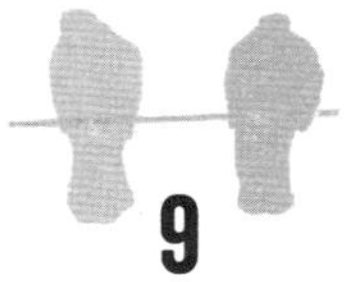

9

FAILURE

It doesn't matter how competent you are, how well you prepare, how well you execute, how improvisational you are, or even how resourceful you are, failure at some point is inevitable. This is no less true with these highly effective people we have talked with in justice ministry. Defeat awaits. The best plans, the most rigorous pursuits, and the most faithful commitments sometimes seem to come to nothing. When this happens, the next step is answering the question, "What do I do now?" This is one of the most important things we can learn from the micro practices of these clergy.

God Uses Our Screw-ups

"When things don't work, what are you to do?" This is the question that Jeremy Troxler raised in his interview. His answer was complex, but he thinks his failures are sometimes the work of the grace of God. He says that he will often go for a walk and then suddenly understand what to do. He sees this as part of the refining process. Circumstances rearrange themselves, and he senses a new direction. Often, he sees that he had it wrong to start with, and that a failure was necessary on the way to discerning what needed to be done. He has great confidence in the grace of God and holds to the belief that ultimately, as he says, "Things are going to work out." He tells me, "God uses our screw-ups" . . . as long as we don't give up.

Troxler is also convinced that "justice is more durable than injustice." While recognizing "the sheer cussedness and outlandishness of evil," he is convinced that "evil eventually destroys itself. It is built on sand." In contrast, "Goodness and love don't do that; they are more durable and lasting." He then claims, "Some days, not giving up is 80 percent of justice." With that he became reflective about the polarization and conflict in his denomination over LGBTQ+ rights. Troxler then quoted a friend of his who said, "Right now in The United Methodist Church, I'm just asking for daily bread. When I need it, there will be some little thing. God will keep me at it, and I didn't ask for it."

In this interview with Troxler, notice that in many of these things he is talking to himself. One may very well question if these are *practices* or something more like internal, subjective, remonstrative *experiences*. Let me suggest instead that they are internal gymnastics in a positive sense of the term. These truly are micro practices that not only remind him of ways he has responded in the past but are durable recitations that have guided him faithfully and effectively through failure into a new future. As he and I talked, I thought of these practices as forms of ritual, of liturgy that enable him to deal with failure and keep going. It is also clear that these are not only found in his internal talks to himself, which can be very important as a micro practice, but also that he shares these things with others, which is evident in quoting his friend about The United Methodist Church.

Fired and Starting Over

Holly McKissick had served the visionary, progressive church she founded for twenty-one years when things "blew up" in 2011. She needed to discipline a popular staff member, a situation that compounded the stress inherent in a rapidly growing church embarking on a third building project while the country was still anxious from the recession. After a process that lasted three months, the church board asked the pastoral staff to resign. McKissick refused and was fired. She was hurt, but the very next day, she called The United Church of Christ conference minister and asked if she could start a new church.

Moving from a suburban location, she founded Peace Church, a UCC/Disciples of Christ congregation in midtown Kansas City. Throughout this ministry, McKissick worked to develop "an open-minded, open-hearted Christian community." She participates in a dizzying number of local service, justice, and community organizing groups: Operation Breakthrough, Big Brothers, Big Sisters, Lead To Read, Stand Up KC, Jobs with Justice, and The Metro Organization for Racial and Economic Equity. Previously she has worked with the board of directors for the Midwest Innocence Project, Planned Parenthood, and the Midwest Center for Holocaust Education.

Along the way, McKissick was challenged and comforted by a rich circle of colleagues. As she had always done, she looked to faithful older clergy for guidance. She intentionally sought a mentor who—along with her therapist, friends, and congregants—ushered her through a period of honest self-reflection. To her daily regimen of running, she added yoga and gardening.

In the end, the devastating loss of the church she founded launched her into a creative ministry far deeper than she could have imagined. "Having come through an experience that nearly killed me," she reports, her preaching "became bolder and freer." Her relationships—from her parents to her parishioners to the poor—took on a more vibrant, authentic shape.

Escape, Sex, Disruption, Contraband, and Walk Outs

Stanley E. Basler, whom we met earlier, began a highly innovative women's prison ministry in Oklahoma. Part of that work was the development of a church that brought prison inmates onto the premises of a local church. Basler wanted to address "a chasm that separated the church door and the prison gate and thought that the church should build a bridge."[45]

Naming this new group "Redemption Church" seemed appropriate "as a vehicle for [offering] redeeming grace to outcasts." Working with the Penn Avenue UMC and the Oklahoma State Department of Corrections, they began meetings at the church with inmates on Sunday afternoons and Thursday evenings. These two meetings included celebration of the Eucharist at every service, an emphasis on worship and membership, working with the notion of base communities out of liberation theology, and reading the Bible through the eyes of the oppressed—all of which were employed as what was envisioned as a "high demand" church.

There were clear successes. They had the support of the UMC annual conference, the department of corrections, and the Penn Avenue Church. They recruited local volunteers and mentors for the program. They performed skits with inmates in acting roles. A choir was organized made up mostly of inmates. Free concerts and a children's program were provided. They worked with the extended families of prisoners, and they established a food pantry. Things had gone so well that in 1998 the department of corrections allowed the program to become coed. Carefully picking the first thirteen men to participate, Basler reports that "these men actually raised the behavior bar. At first, they were better than the women."[46]

And there were clear failures. The church's first pastor, a convicted sex offender in Kansas who claimed innocence, became sexually involved with a married male ex-prisoner. He resigned, and his wife, who was the church musician, divorced him. The second pastor, an Episcopalian with dreams of priesthood, was a flamboyant speaker with a good personality. But after a few months he was found to be having an affair with a woman and hence resigned.

There were a few, not many, prisoner escapes. The rest room in the church became a site for passing along contraband and for sexual action, as did the furnace room on one occasion when an inmate picked the lock. The alley wall of the church outside became known as "lovers' lane," a place for hugging and kissing, which lead one neighbor to call a local TV news station asking them to film what was going on. There was also an unsigned letter sent to the governor that was, as Basler says, "complaining and exaggerating what was happening."

Added to all of this was disruption in worship, including times when people would just get up and leave. In response, the staff developed practices of confrontation, write-ups of infractions, and exclusions of some participants, but these were never finally effective or satisfying. Even increasing the ratio of volunteers to inmates—at first from one-to-eight and then from one-to-five—was not the answer. At one time, the program had two hundred inmates in attendance, which was too many and unmanageable. They tried hosting multiple services, but that was still too many. And then, conversely, in 2019 and 2020, the department of corrections would not let inmates out to church because of the pandemic. As in many other churches, the attendance never recovered.

But they did learn from their mistakes. For one thing, they simply had to work with smaller numbers. The program added a second church in Oklahoma, so that there was the original church in Oklahoma City and now a new Redemption Church in Lawton working with inmates. Second, the state of Oklahoma itself ended its Community Corrections Centers for Women, the source of women for the Redemption Churches, which meant that the church program would be working now only with men, which reduced the population mass. Further, leaders of the church program realized that the ratios of staff/volunteers to inmates had to be even lower, and a one-to-four ratio became the standard for the work.

In addition, they developed a program called Exodus House, which describes itself on its website as "a faith based, residential program established for the purpose of equipping released ex-prisoners and their families to become productive, self-supporting, cohesive family units."[47] These multi-family residences require two full-time staff who live on-site, and most of the staff are ex-prisoners themselves. Volunteers also continue to be active in this program. Further, upon graduation, Exodus residents get their savings and the contents of the apartment, including furniture, towels, dishes, and silverware. Basler reports, "Twice in our history we admitted two different men, each with physical custody of four children. That means someone determined that these two men coming straight from prison were the best situation for these children." Also, on two occasions that Basler knows of, a judge sentenced someone to Exodus House. And Basler concludes, "I truly believe Exodus House is the Cadillac of re-entry housing ministry in Oklahoma."

When I look at the challenge Basler and The United Methodist Church faced in Redemption Church and, later, Exodus House, I am amazed they stuck with this effort. I think particularly of an array of practices that were engaged in this work: telephone conversations, personal contacts, one-on-ones, small group meetings, working with the department of corrections, recruiting, training, and staying in touch with volunteers, connecting with local churches, initiating and keeping relationships with their local district of The United Methodist Church, ongoing interactions with inmates, touching base, and following up with people across the entire field of this work. It is simply mind blowing.

While it is easy to focus on the struggles of the program and its failures, it would be a mistake to miss the many small practices and the developing skills they represented in this remarkable work. I am impressed as well by the trial-and-error dimension of this work, the ways Basler and this range of people continued to try new things for years on end. There are plenty of times in our lives when we face circumstances where we don't know the way out, but the practices of trial and error surely must be one way we do, from time to time, find the way through that God offers.

Crack Houses, Setbacks, and Grants

Joseph Daniels Jr. advises justice-ministry workers, "Don't be discouraged by setbacks; setbacks open the door for other things God will do." He then told me the following story. Near the church were two apartment buildings that were in tax court. They had been crack houses, and the congregation wanted to redevelop these buildings into affordable housing. They put together a 2.7-million-dollar grant proposal, but their competition was another community organization that had ties with the city council, and their project was chosen instead. "We learned from this that there were relationships we had not built," Daniels said.

It was a tough disappointment, but someone in the church told Daniels to have hope, saying, "Don't get down, let's do the next thing." So, they purchased another house down the street and transformed the current church parsonage into their first housing facility. This began the process through which they developed a grant that led to a sixty-million-dollar project.

Now, Emory Church is surrounded by a large development of affordable housing that they have rebuilt or constructed. They have a 180,000 square-foot multipurpose campus called Beacon Center that is at the forefront of their mission. Its community-based programs are "designed to be the catalyst to help community members reach their full potential." These community-based programs are undergirded by locations for art, culture, and music, and further include a gymnasium, classrooms, food pantry, immigration clinics and small business services. Soon the center will develop a commercial restaurant with "returning citizens" as its employees. Also in the offing are a second community kitchen, a youth leadership academy, and a health clinic. In the end, a 2.7-million-dollar failed proposal led to a sixty-million-dollar success, all because of hope.

In the last ten years or so, I have become convinced that hope is not a subjective, positive, mental state, but is more accurately and powerfully understood as a micro practice. Hope is identity, being someone you would not otherwise be; hope is location, being in a place you would not otherwise go; hope is engagement, taking on things you would not otherwise challenge; hope is action, standing up to the principalities and powers and standing with the dispossessed, the marginalized, and the excluded. Its mandate is Mary's Magnificat (Luke 1:46-55); its most expansive and widespread enactment is in the ordinary, in the mundane, in the living out of a new and different way of being so the world can be transformed.

The Spirituality of Failure

Michael Zedek told a story about his attempt to add an eight o'clock Sabbath service to follow the usual early evening service at his synagogue. He assumed that the earlier service made it difficult for people to get there on time after a busy day. But the new time was "an absolute failure." Two years later, though, young adults asked for the second service, and it became a success. Zedek's takeaway was, "It is easier to meet needs that it is to create them."

This story led him to reflections about the struggles he had when he first entered the rabbinate. He was worried both that he would not be a success but also that he was not interested in the corporate definition of success. In this time of restlessness, the word came to him, "What makes you think you should be a better failure than Moses?" With this question he thought about being true to the vision that we are called to be faithful, not successful. He pointed out what Deuteronomy 16:20 says about righteousness, that we must pursue justice. Zedek says this should be read as "justly you shall persist." Zedek is saying that your message, your means, and your avenues of seeking righteousness must be just in themselves. The means we use are to be intrinsic to the ends we seek.

Recognizing that he was not the Messiah—he said laughing—led him to the idea that the rabbinate was better understood in terms of the role of the enabler. He then quoted Saul Alinsky's iron rule of organizing, "Never do for others what they can do for themselves." He used two examples. One, if he is invited to dedicate a home, his answer is, "No, but I will come and help you to do so." A second example is when invited to come and say a few words for an event, he invites others to speak as well. Zedek then told me about *zimzum*, a Hebrew term that originates in the Kabbalah and refers to God's contraction of Godself before the creation of the world for the purpose of creating the world.[48] Or, as Zedek explains, "That time where God steps back and lets others shine." In illustration, he tells the story of a

Midwest meeting of congregations in his synagogue. Throughout the day, he sat in his pulpit, but never said a word. At the end of the day, one of his colleagues stated, "You do nothing better than anybody else in the rabbinate"—high praise in that context.

I then asked Zedek if there was a question he wished I had raised with him. "Yes," he answered immediately. "What's the right way to be wrong?" He went on to answer, "I can live with myself if I have loved too much, but not if I have cared too little."

At that point he observed that he has always been more concerned with making connections than with outcomes. Further, he quoted the Mishnah sage Rabbi Tarfon: "You are not obligated to finish the task, but neither are you free to desist from it." He also mentioned a central principle in Judaism, *tikkun olam,* that translates as "repair the world." He next paraphrased a comment by the American writer E. B. White, "I wake up every morning torn between the desire to savor the world and the desire to save it." Zedek added his concern about "people who work for justice who have no joy and those into joy who have no concern for justice."

He next discussed the difference between rewards and what is important in the work of justice. Zedek has a penchant for offering two or three sharply contrasting stories to make his point. He spoke of Red Buttons—who made a comedic career with the phrase "Never got a dinner!"—talking about people who made important contributions but never got recognized with a benefit. From this Zedek moved quickly to Lenny Bruce, who said something like, "Any clergyman who has more than one suit, where a third of the world is starving, is a hypocrite." Amid these stories and comments, he quoted Oscar Wilde to the effect that there's only one thing worse in this world than not getting what you want. That's getting it.

Zedek spoke of how much he already has, quoting a rabbi who said, "My life is blessed because I never needed what I did not already have." With that, he recommended *The Spirituality of Imperfection: Storytelling and the Search for Meaning* by Ernest Kurtz and Katherine Ketcham Looking back through his comments, I am struck by both the realism and the challenge of a spirituality of imperfection.

Successor Failure

One matter that came up in the interviews several times was the failure of a successor in the work these interviewees had begun. In other words, a creative, innovative, effective job of justice ministry was diminished or ended entirely when put into someone else's hands. I will not name the clergy I interviewed or their successors, but important research could be done on micro practices that led to the failure of a successor. And, of course, discovering small practices that ensure the effectiveness of a successor would be even more valuable.

Based on these interviews, let me name four best practices in this regard. The first is to begin planning for a successor at least a year ahead of time. This planning has both formal and informal procedures. It needs, for example, an official group of people in the church to begin anticipating the change and planning for the right person to come. How this is done will vary according to denominational policies, but even in an appointment system, there is still planning that can be carried out and important conversations to be had with the church, its ministries, and denominational leadership. This, of course, means conversations and serious listening to the people participating in the congregation and in its ministries.

Second, careful evaluation needs to be done of the strengths and weaknesses of the present pastor. This does not have to be hurtful, but it is important to think about the gifts, graces, and skills of the pastor that are evident in the program's success, as well as areas that can be improved. Both need to be factored into the search for the successor.

Third, if possible, get the successor pastor into key meetings of the church and its ministry while the outgoing pastor is still serving. This is important for continuity of leadership. None of this obviates the need for innovation and creativity from the new pastor. Rather, a new pastor must be able to extend what has been effectively done while offering corrective directions for what can and will be done in the future.

Finally, and most important, a gracious exit that is relatively free of egoism is one of the most significant contributions a pastor can make to ministry in that church. Conversely, few things are sadder than pastors so captured with self-importance that they not only fail to contribute to the future of this justice ministry but set back forward progress by hurting the work in motion.

10

INFLUENCES, MENTORS, AND ANCESTORS

Parents, Etiquette, and Integrity

The first thing Doug Alpert said in our interview was that he constantly gives credit to those on whose shoulders he stands, especially his parents. His father was a public person who spent his career in real estate and worked for equity in housing. He took pride in taking care of his employees, paying them well and providing benefits. He respected work of any kind. And Alpert's mother would have been a social worker if she had lived in another generation. People came to see her with their problems; she listened to and empathized with them. Alpert says his influences start with his mother.

In an aside, Alpert observed, "People don't want you to solve their problems; they just want to be heard." Regarding his work as a rabbi, he says, "It is all about one-on-ones, about being accessible and not beyond reach. I want to be interested in and to care about their lives."

He then turned to etiquette. "I learned from my family to always say 'please' and 'thank you,'" he reflects. "On the opposite side of the coin," Alpert says, "people who champion justice externally but treat their own workers like crap internally draw my ire." Alpert also told me that custodial work at his synagogue, while not in his job description, is part of his work there, and that he appreciates that kind of work and the workers who do it. Growing up, he and his friends all held working-class jobs. Alpert's father put a broom and dustpan in his hand as a young teenager and instructed him to clean up after drywall workers.

It can hardly be missed in this part of my interview with Alpert that the influences on him reside so significantly in practices he witnessed and was formed by. His father was a public person who treated employees right, and his mother was an unofficial social worker who helped people with their problems. Alpert's family was committed to the dignity of work and to the little things of etiquette and their significance. Alpert's interview is testimony to the important influence of micro practices of justice in that close range of parental character and action and in childhood relationships and concrete, lived experience.

Newspapers, Family, Mentors, and Story

When Emanuel Cleaver II was nine years old, one of his teachers told his class that they should read the newspaper every day. Shortly after that, he was talking with his father and told him that he would like to get the newspaper every morning. His father told him they couldn't afford it. The discussion was closed, but his father looked at the Lucky Strike he was smoking and realized that smoking cost more than the local paper; he immediately went to the bathroom and dropped his cigarettes in the toilet. After that, when the paper would come to the house, Cleaver would beat everybody outside to get it. So, beginning when he was nine years old, he could talk about the Eisenhower administration, and he read everything he could find about the civil rights movement. Cleaver commented that reading the newspaper every day in Wichita Falls, Texas, did not give him all the news. Later, in other print sources he would read about civil rights activist Fred Shuttlesworth and about his cousin Eldridge Cleaver, whose book *Soul on Ice* would have significant impact on Emanuel Cleaver's young life.

Reading the news was key for Cleaver because it made him aware of what was going on around him. Even so, he says, "It was not enough to know about it, you had to be involved in it." In 1959 at age fifteen, he led a civil rights march. Today, he regularly reads *The New York Times*, *The Kansas City Star*, *The Washington Post*, *The Wall Street Journal*, *USA Today*, and *The Economist*. So, reading the newspaper has remained a micro practice of over sixty years. He said, "I have taken Karl Barth seriously where he says that you have to have the newspaper in one hand and the Bible in the other."

To be sure, people like his father were important in his development. His mother, Marie Cleaver, was a campaign manager for others who ran for office. "She would get out on the street talking to people." She had courage, too. In her small Texas town, she had once ordered a hamburger, Coke, and fries at a local café, and the manager told her she had to eat the meal outside. She got up and left the meal and the establishment without paying.

Cleaver also noted the importance of his marriage to the former Dianne Donaldson, who is as committed to social justice and activism as he is. Further, he spoke of his daughter and reports, "I can call her, and she can tell me about everything that's in the news."

Desperately important as well was Cleaver's early engagement with the civil rights movement and some of its top leaders. He mentions that James Lawson, John Lewis, Fred Shuttlesworth, Joe Lowry, and Ralph Abernathy included him in their group early on. Major Jones, then president of Gammon Theological Seminary—the only historically Black seminary of The United Methodist Church—invited him to enroll there, saying, "Boy, you come down here. You come with me, and I'm gonna train you!" But Cleaver was dating the future Mrs. Cleaver at the time and remained in Kansas City. Still, he continued to work with this group of civil rights leaders.

As a result, he and John Nettles, later the vice president of the Southern Christian Leadership Conference (SCLC), became the youth movement of that organization. Reflecting on some of the internecine conflict of the time and differences of strategy and tactics, Cleaver said in an aside, "Hanging out with the SCLC got me in trouble with SNCC" (the Student Nonviolent Coordinating Committee). Cleaver also reflected something of his sensitivity to ego problems that can possess a civil rights leader. He quoted Martin Luther King Jr. as characterizing one nationally known leader of the movement this way: "The cameras had taken control of his life."

Cleaver eventually founded and became the executive of the Kansas City Southern Christian Leadership Conference. Responding to the call to ministry, he entered Saint Paul School of Theology and in 1972 became pastor of Saint James UMC, where he served until 2009.

There was also an important development theologically for Cleaver. Half of the clergy in his family had been Church of God in Christ, and Cleaver declared that "they had a horrible theology of homosexuality." But Cleaver had had a gay cousin who would sometimes put on the high heels of the girls in the family. Nobody thought much about it until one day a guy called him a sissy. "That was my first street fight," Cleaver interjected. "My cousin hardened my theology for championing everybody."

As an adult, this same cousin joined the First African Methodist Episcopal Church in Los Angeles and became active in the choir. But soon after, the pastor called and told him that some of the men did not want him singing in the choir, and he was kicked out, which devastated him. From that time until he died, Cleaver's cousin wrote notes about how much the church meant to him and how that exclusion had been personally destructive. Cleaver and the family did not know about this event and his cousin's reflections on it until they read the notes after his death. Cleaver concluded, "This issue is no longer just an intellectual enterprise for me."

He went on to say that "both Joe Lowry and Major Jones worked on me. They helped me with my theology. Joe Lowry told me, 'You can't be for justice if you are just for Black people. You must separate your beliefs from the Ku Klux Klan. Don't be exclusive the way the KKK is.'"

After my conversation with Cleaver, I felt that I wanted more from him on micro practices of pastoring his church, serving city offices, and working as a congressman. But as I began going through our interview, I saw how it was populated with micro practices. I thought of the connection he made between reading the paper and social action, even at age fifteen. It was hard to miss the role of people like his father, his mother, James Lawson, John Lewis, Fred Shuttlesworth, Joe Lowery, Ralph Abernathy, Major Jones, and his wife Dianne. And one must not overlook how his cousin's struggle against homophobia affected Cleaver's theology and inclusive understanding of justice for everyone. I think of the hundreds—probably thousands—of face-to-face meetings he had with all these people, in addition to the day-to-day, ordinary conversations with them and many others. I'm awed by their impact on his life and the ever-expanding range of relationships and practices that grew out of these formative experiences.

I also realized how much Cleaver thinks in stories. I have known him more than fifty years and have heard him speak many times. I have never heard him make a speech or deliver a sermon without a story. In fact, I have never had a conversation with him for more than three minutes without hearing a story. He has a narrative mind. It is the way he thinks. It is a major theological and political tool of the first order that is at his command and serves him very well. It is a practice he uses in one-on-ones, small groups, large meetings, sermons, and other speeches. Look back through our interview and see that his comments are an ongoing chronicle of events that illuminate and typically make the case for the point or the agenda he is advancing. I do not mean to suggest that he does not marshal data, research, and information for his position, but rather that these are typically presented in anecdotes or tales or quotidian episodes, something he does very well.

Family, Scripture, Authors, and the People

We previously met Joel Martinez in our discussions on doing change. Here we turn to the influences that have shaped his life. He began our interview by stating that family is "our first home, our first community, our first formation of school in Christian and spiritual life. We must find a way to honor and respect family and its role in our lives." He describes pastors (especially United Methodist pastors) as itinerants. "We move and we need a sensitivity about how our own families have had to adjust to different places not of their own choosing." His wife, Rachel, and their kids went with the flow of his assignments. Without them and their willingness to move, he could not have done much. He notes, also, that a family needs to be rooted in deep respect for their heritage. To be gifted with a knowledge of that heritage is an enormous blessing.

Martinez also spoke of the role of scripture and prayer and of reading for his pastoral and spiritual life. He said he could not have dealt with life in the ministry in the eighties without the books of Rueben Job and W. Paul Jones. Further, the lectionary and the themes of the Christian year held him and his family together. And he spoke of "the rhythm given to life by sacred moments" of meditation and prayer, "without which we all burn out."

Crucial, too, are the wisdom, the sensitivity, and the gifts of others. "You need to be informed by them. Your fountain alone won't give you enough water." He continued, "Your authority comes from beyond you. It comes from the pew." He illustrated this with the way he conducts funerals. When he preaches, Martinez "works his way down to sit with the family of the person being remembered." He will say to these family mourners, "I come from the pew, from you, the people." He then reminds them that they cultivate the people that God calls. He further states that "some of the most gifted people are the laity, and listening to the work of the Spirit among the people" is of the first order of importance.

Accountability Circles and Ancestors

Each of the pastors I interviewed dealt with the issue of influences differently, something that each contributed in a different and distinctive way. Janet Wolf spoke of influences both in the present and in the past—of people, but also of art. She began by speaking of accountability and the very important part that community plays in this regard. She requires a community that will hold her accountable and at the same time move her out of her location. For this reason, she participates in circles inside prison. In our chapter on theology Wolf spoke of practicing resurrection. She finds that people she meets in prison practice resurrection because "they are living in defiance of death against such huge odds." She is also part of the National Council of Elders, a group she characterizes as "nonviolent organizers from the twentieth century who have not given up."

She emphasizes again how essential it is to be based in community. She meets with women once a week to be "rooted in a different vision." They gather around potlucks with pictures on the walls of people who are not like her, people "whose lives are different than mine, who remind me of others, of people who don't look like me." In these gatherings, she says, quoting Emilie Townes, they "listen each other into life." Together, they "wind up in photos, stories, and potlucks, all mixed up." Moving to a different venue, she says, "I work with a man who was caged on death row for twenty-one years, and I believe he's innocent." His photos remind her, "I will never get it right by myself."

She confesses that she too often holds on to chains that keep her in captivity. She admits her need, first, to identify the chains with which she is caught, and second, to let go and find freedom. Here she registers her debt to Dorothee Sölle, a German liberation theologian who helped her recognize these chains and enter three emancipative practices: First is "to practice and be caught up in wonder, to be awakened to the gifts of God's creation and the power of God's presence." Second is to "unlearn the ways of empire, the seduction of consumerism, the web of lies that prop up power and privilege and let go." And the third practice is "to resist in order to heal and heal in order to resist, as individuals and communities." She elaborates this point in her book: "We can heal through resistance and 'change death-oriented reality.'"[49]

In these community groups, those in the circle help each other toward a different conception of justice. Everything is valued through the lens of the good life, attempting "to find harmony with all the pieces of creation." It is a new form of existence that is rooted in a theology of abundance, not scarcity. It is a justice-seeking, life-giving *Dayenu*, which is Hebrew for "it would have been enough."[50] That is, what we have is sufficient. It is far better to be grateful for what we have than to complain about what we do not.

Wolf says she sometimes meditates by bending her knees, scooping up the love all around, pulling it down onto herself, and then splashing the abundance of love back out into the universe. Wolf follows this comment immediately by saying, "Then my mom and dad who died several years ago are present with me, and I am reminded of the abundant love that surrounds me, us, always." She becomes aware of "a cloud of witnesses." In these moments she writes the names of specific people she is trying to listen to. She will pick up rocks representing specific people, or ribbons or stuff that remind her of people who can challenge her. These witnesses, these ancestors, are crucial ongoing influences on her life. In relationship to them she says, "I have had amazing opportunities. On my own, I would get it wrong."

In this context she quotes Philip Gourevitch that power is "the ability to force others to inhabit your story of their reality."[51] Wolf realizes that this happened to her when she was a single mom with two boys and working three part-time jobs: The powerful silence of her story put her "into their [her employers'] version of my reality." She even claims, "They were not intentionally dismissive. They were trying to help me, but they could not break through the walls of their own economic security and assumptions in ways that allowed them to really see or hear me." She then made the point again of the importance of one's location and of those we are related to. If we are not "in ongoing partnership with marginalized communities," we will have the "luxury of distance," a captivity that separates us from life.[52]

Wolf often speaks of music and other forms of art and creativity that shape her. She collects paintings from Nicaragua, South Africa, Haiti, and death row. In every room of her house, she has pieces of art that represent influences on her life and witness. She says that

Walter Wink's book *Unmasking the Powers* saved her life by helping her unmask, name, challenge, and transform the powers. In her own book she used the following observation by Barbara Brown Taylor: "Sin is collective; the systems do our sinning for us." In our interview, Wolf clarified that point: "The system shapes what goes down."

That is nowhere clearer than in prison, where she strives to train people in transformative justice. Further, she works in freedom schools where the scholars and kids learn to uncover their gifts, their history, and their culture. Crucial to her work is the commitment of "not making things separate from other people." For Wolf, "there are no lines between justice and anything else." All the pieces of one's life come together around justice and love. This means art and poetry and music and creativity are all paramount for the work of justice.

Looking back over our interview, I am staggered by the complexities of the influences on her life in the work of justice and how filled these are with micro practices. She joins communities of accountability, surrounds herself with art that witnesses to her, and works in prisons and freedom schools. She is committed to a release from the powers and to building a close connection between resistance and healing. Wolf is working to re-conceptualize justice through a range of face-to-face practices to enact harmony in the gathering together of the pieces of creation, and to recognize and engage ancestors even as we become forebears ourselves.

Holy Clowns and Black Female Jesus

Born to a low-income family of nine children, including three sets of twins—of which he and his identical twin, Darrell, were the last—Bill

Breeden was raised in the holiness tradition and started preaching in revivals at the age of fifteen. The evangelistic team included a gospel quartet, and Breeden's expectation was to continue in that tradition as an evangelist after high school. However, his Selective Service draft number was fifteen, and his mother already had three sons in the military with one off the coast of Vietnam. She insisted that her twin boys enroll in college as ministerial students, providing them with a draft deferment.

His "Damascus Road" experience was in an alley behind the supermarket where he worked his first year of college in Nashville. He told me, "Being the newbie on the workforce, I got the shit jobs. All the employees were White, 90 percent of the customers Black. The store was on the edge of the African American ghetto." One of those jobs was burning the old food and trash every night. Having been poor but never hungry and having lived for the first eighteen years of his life near an Indiana "sundown town" (White towns/municipalities that excluded people of color at dusk), Breeden came face to face with his own inherent racism and fear of people of color.

At one o'clock one morning at the grocery store, he was loading the incinerator in the alley behind the store to burn the outdated food and trash when a voice said, "If you leave the matches, I'll start the fire. You threw some cheese in there, and I want it. It helps me feed my kids." She was Black, and Breeden was afraid there were others behind her. Breeden says he then realized that he did not know there were hungry people in America. He had thought that hungry people were just lazy. But as he looked at that woman, the words of Jesus in Matthew 25:40 came to him, "Whatever you did for one of the least of these brothers and sisters of mine, you did for me" (NIV). He never learned her name but identified her in our interview as his "Black Female Jesus." His long-practiced religiosity no longer made sense, and thus began his "spiritual journey to wholeness."

With the Vietnam War going on, Breeden was ashamed at first that he couldn't fight. It wasn't so much that he was afraid to fight, but that he was trying to figure out war. He then read Kurt Vonnegut's *Slaughterhouse Five.* It showed him that war is a disaster. Breeden said, "I still honor those who serve—they have good intentions—but intentions don't work."

Breeden served in parish ministry for six years in the Christian Church (Disciples of Christ). Then on December 7, 1979, he hitchhiked through a winter storm from St. Joseph, Missouri, to Louisville, Kentucky, and encountered the radical Christianity of Philip Berrigan. He once again had to face the contradictions of his life. He and his courageous wife, Glenda, decided to leave the middle class and seek a simpler life and work for peace.

Breeden was eventually given the title of "Holy Clown" by Vonnegut himself for his actions during the Iran-Contra affair (discussed earlier in this book), which Breeden termed "nonviolent guerrilla street theater." He also made two trips from Bloomington, Indiana, to Polsetega, Nicaragua, and spent time in a Honduran prison, as he reported previously.

In 2001, Breeden became a co-minister of the Unitarian Universalist Church of Bloomington, Indiana. There he pastored with Mary Ann Macklin, a lesbian, and the church grew from around 250 members to about 500. Breeden retired in 2014 and has since been working on his memoirs entitled, "Billy Pilgrim and the Black Female Jesus."

Quite frankly, Bill Breeden's life is a full-blown mystery to me. How do you come out of the evangelical-holiness tradition as a teenage preacher; become transformed by an encounter with a "Black Female Jesus"; find yourself roiled by the Vietnam War and this country's illicit activity in Nicaragua; take it upon yourself to steal the street sign in your hometown named after a prominent national politician and propose a ransom of $30 million for its return; then live on a survival income with your family in a teepee and a cabin made of junk; and then return to parish ministry for fourteen years as an effective co-pastor with a lesbian colleague in a growing Unitarian Universalist church before returning to rural acreage in southern Indiana? It blows my mind! Yet, notice how few macro practices are involved in the story. See how much of it occurs in face-to-face moments that then lead to extraordinary things.

11

CONFLICT, CONTROVERSY, AND CONFRONTATION

Dealing with Christians and Bacon

I asked Doug Alpert about the difficulties of being a Jew and a rabbi in interfaith settings. He admitted that it can be a problem. In the past year, one of the community organizing efforts in Kansas City held a breakfast bringing together labor union membership and religious leaders. The union's caterer made a sumptuous table of fruit, biscuits, eggs, and meat. The problem was that the cooks had mixed bacon with the eggs. There was no kosher option.

During the evaluation of the meeting, Alpert said, "If this is a Christian affair, then well and good, but if this is an interfaith gathering, then we need to respect the traditions that are present." Of course, we Christians should've said it, and certainly that menu will not happen again. But, still, there it is, just one more example of a failure to be sensitive to other faith traditions. I was there, and I am embarrassed to say that I was so preoccupied with seating and arrangements that I didn't even notice.

So, I asked Alpert how he handles similar situations in other settings. He reports that he is often the only rabbi and frequently the only Jew in the room, so he is careful to pick and choose when to point out situations that would marginalize him. He says, "My primary purpose for being involved with organizations working for justice is to support others, and not necessarily to press a Jewish agenda. I have other spaces to do that. When I do bring up situations that are marginalizing, I do so not to critique but rather to see an opportunity for a teaching moment." With a trace of humor, he adds, "I like being the only rabbi in the room. There is no other rabbi there to contradict me."

Albert spoke particularly of events in which an interpretation of scripture will be from a decidedly Christian point of view that presents Jews or Pharisees (read rabbis) as examples of what not to do who are then shown up by Jesus. In situations like these, he tries to be assertive, to be measured, and to speak up at the right time. Further, he concedes that he likes to work with Christians, to be himself in the same space, and to give Christians the opportunity to get to know him. He said, "There's a way to be honest without being a dick about it."

"It does require a form of disciplined practice and mindfulness," he inserted. "You have to be alert to things like bacon in the eggs." He then used this observation to expand his comments with respect to other people. For example, he spoke of relating to secular Jews, especially young adults who tend to identify with Judaism but see a disconnect between their values and Jewish institutions. So, in this case, Alpert sees the institutional piece as different. As one example, recognizing that most young adults are welcoming and want to relate to the queer community, his congregation works hard to recruit queer Jews to Congregation Kol Ami. (I hasten to say that this is an intrinsic commitment of the Kol Ami community, not merely some means of reaching young adults.) In these efforts, Alpert does many one-on-ones. He wants secular and young adult Jews to get a clearer picture of the synagogue and of the Jewish tradition.

Conflict and a Sense of Humor

In the chapter on doing change, we discussed that Erin Counihan made significant changes in her small church in St. Louis. She would say, "We're going to try something, something new." She acknowledged that this sometimes led to conflict, and she advised that "a sense of humor works, so be funny." She would laugh at herself and admit to the congregation when she made mistakes. They would try new things and use humor in doing so.

Still, people got angry with her. "When people got mad at me, things were hard. I took stands and people were not used to it." She told those with whom she disagreed that she loved them. About one man she reported, "He needed to be mad, and he needed to know I wasn't going to back down." She then recalled that "The Holy Spirit kept my butt in that seat. We stayed in relationship and stayed close. We are still friends." In fact, at Oak Hill Church, "We could try anything the whole time I was there." Yet she also commented, "You also have to do some things that are not controversial, not political. You can't do justice every Sunday!" For example, the congregation loves to have meals together and feed people. But they also examined programs people were not attending and stopped doing them.

Polarities, the Dilemma of Leadership, and Painting with a Brush

The approach of Harold W. Garman to conflict, confrontation, and controversy was quite different but effective. Part of the reason is the context in which he worked, and the other part, as he says, grew out of who he is. He pointed out that he was working in a context with both liberals and conservatives, but that he had enough liberals to keep positive initiatives and programs going.

Basic to his work was to keep these polarities in conversation and working together. His role was to affirm their ideas, to love them, to be involved, and to get resources together. Garman himself tended to take more moderate positions to get people to listen to each other, which seemed crucial in that setting. He also said, "I hailed from a farm, so I was always very practical." He further observed that the situation today is so polarized across the country that his approach may not work now.

As a PhD candidate at Boston University School of Theology in the sixties, he had read J. Milton Yinger's *Religion, Society and the Individual,* which discussed the dilemma of religious leadership: To make a change in a church or religious organization, a leader must move quickly enough and far enough out to keep tension to pull it in a new direction. At the same time, if that leader moves too rapidly or too far out front, it will break the relationship and lose the influence. This teaching meant a great deal to Garman, and he found it important in his work at the church in Syracuse, keeping the tension but not breaking it.

Still, there was more going on here. For example, a Boston coalition developed a program named "10 Points against Gun Violence." So, working with others, Garman helped initiate that program in Syracuse. A major part of that effort was working with local guys and using a boxing center to reduce violence. Garman spent a lot of time listening to and working with these men and teenage boys, getting to know them. After eight years, he asked, "What caused you to trust me for all this time?" One of the Black men said, "You are the only person, Black or White, who had come by and told us the truth. You never promised us something that didn't come true."

The man then added, "Brother Garman, you paint with a brush." Garman elaborated—and don't worry about the mixed metaphors—that this meant that Garman "did not hit them over the head with a ball bat." He took the time to listen, and what the men thought got incorporated "into the painting." The ideas of the men and the youth, the development of the project, and the ongoing shaping of the work occurred together, largely because Garman pulled together the contributions of the participants into the scenery of the larger picture.

Garman worked in a situation like that of many clergy in the US today. The local church is often a mix of the political left and right. His taking a more moderate position to keep these polarities in conversation is a significant approach for working in a context where many clergy find themselves. Note that there is a kind of patience here to work with people across the political spectrum, to continue to listen, and to keep them engaged with each other so that there is a building of consensus that enables people to move into and to continue justice work. Garman's sensitivity to Yinger's leadership dilemma doubtlessly played an important role in being able to sustain congregational support while engaging in outreach programs that build a relationship between the church and the community while sustaining an ethos in the church necessary to that work.

It may seem counterintuitive to begin a boxing program to promote nonviolence, but Garman's commitment to nonviolence is clear. His intense practice of listening led him to recognize the importance of this program. It was very much a part of his "painting with a brush." His incorporation of a variety of scenes promoted by those he encountered made him a faithful artist who displayed the images and visions of the community.

Conflict and Money

When John Flowers gave presentations on church revitalization to local congregations and clergy and laity seminars, he repeatedly got asked, "What's the most important thing you have to know?" His answer was: "You have to be able to watch money walk out the door." He tells the story of one Sunday school class at Travis Park UMC that took its class picture off the wall and marched out at 10:55 a.m., right before Sunday morning worship, taking permanent leave of the church. Someone said to Flowers, "That's sixty thousand dollars walking out the door." He said, "You have to be immune to losing money."

This means finding money in other places, of course, and finding additional resources. He knows that the city council, the city manager, and other elected people must give money away by law. So, he got to know who those people were and found appropriate ways to solve their problems by matching their funding with his programs.

For instance, Flowers noted that the downtown police were a bicycle patrol. Dealing with homeless people was 75 to 80 percent of their job. So Flowers was able to get money for bicycles for homeless people, whom they called "behavioral specialists," and who would ride around outside and build relationships with other homeless people. Flowers notes that this cut down on the work of the police and built connections among the homeless.

However, Flowers did raise a caution about getting social services involved. He has often found that governmental agencies have the idea that churches would deliver services but not actually engage the poor and homeless. Flowers insisted, instead, that "These are humans. We must build relationships with them, and we have to ask the question, 'Who is the human being in front of me?'" And then we must respond.

Flowers had one last story about finding resources. One Sunday morning, he noticed a homeless man painting his shoes black. He asked why and was told, "You have to have black shoes to get a job." But it turned out that the man's shoes were a little tight, so Flowers gave him his shoes and later led worship in his socks. It just so happened that Shane Claiborne, a Christian activist and leading figure in the New Monasticism movement, was the guest preacher that morning and made a comment about this action by Flowers. When it came time for the Eucharist, people came forward and placed their shoes on the communion table.

I am impressed by the sheer ingenuity of Flowers's approach to justice ministry. He is innovative. He's ready to lose money. For him, the homeless people are not the problem; the system is. And he turns problems into programs. He is fearless, but it gets expressed in widening the focus of his attention. It is not merely turning lemons into lemonade; he transubstantiates conflict and difficulty into opening a new future, and most of these moves by him are micro escapades that involve face-to-face encounters with church members, public officials, hotel managers, the police, and homeless people.

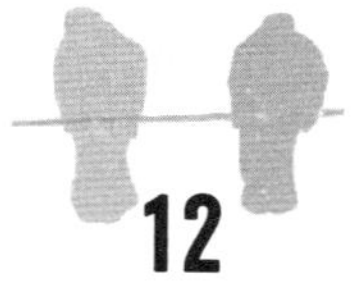

12

PRISON MINISTRY AND DOING TIME

The Whipsaws of Prison Ministry

Paul Witmer is lead pastor of Women at the Well, a United Methodist Church in the Iowa Correctional Institution for Women in Mitchellville, Iowa. Reflecting on his own micro practices, he thought first of spiritual practices. In the formative part of his spirituality, he had been drawn to silence, solitude, and spiritual retreats like the Walk to Emmaus. These influences have stayed with him across the years. He has practiced Centering Prayer now for twenty-five years, to which he devotes twenty minutes a day—sometimes twice a day—three times per week.

Naming his own micro practices, he said next that showing up is crucial in prison ministry. He also used the word ***networking*** to describe this practice. After coming to Women at the Well, he became involved with reentry, the process of bringing former inmates back into the wider society, a ministry that requires a lot of relationships all over Iowa. You need to be present in many places to get to know people across the state. "You need to show up in court and in meetings with law-enforcement people, social workers, and others."

At this point, he admitted he was an introvert and that it is not easy for him to meet people, but, he said, "I just go." He remembered going to meet with the head of the department of corrections in Iowa. He found it hard to do, but when he got there, he discovered that the department head was the son of a United Methodist pastor. That made building that relationship a lot easier.

He confesses that he shows up at meetings that "bore the hell out of me," but he acknowledges it is important face time, and that there are often important players there. Estimating that 85 percent of these meetings are a waste of time, nevertheless these meetings have given him a network people across the state he can call on and who can call on him.

The Iowa Interfaith Alliance is another place to show up. The Alliance organized Faithful Voices, which meets on Wednesday of every week around issues of racial justice. Again, sometimes these meetings are boring. Because Black pastors are often overworked and underpaid and there are not many Muslim participants, it is mostly just White people, but they are active. He noted that the state legislature is now actively harming LGBTQ+ people and promoting racist policies. So, it is important for these voices to be raised up and to call the legislature into question. They make phone calls, send emails, and go to forums to discuss these issues with more open legislators.

He then makes the point that women prisoners are quite different from male inmates and cannot be treated like men. He reports that 95 percent of women at Iowa Correctional Institution for Women, where he serves, are survivors of trauma, largely sexual assault. For the broader community of women experiencing incarceration, which includes jail, parole, or probation (commonly known as community based corrections), this number rises to 98 percent.[53] The traumas are the result of physical and sexual abuse. This condition requires responses unique to women, Witmer maintains.

Because of this awareness, the church's staff tries to be sensitive to trauma, not speak harshly to people, and operate in collaborative, cooperative ways. The congregational model at work also attempts to develop leadership among the women. Witmer reported that one woman was invited back to share her experience after twenty-nine years in the prison. She said, "This prison is not a very sisterly place, and this church gave me the sisterhood I needed." Witmer emphasized the importance of finding congregational community in the prison, suggesting that a woman can use what learns about church in prison when she gets outside.

He did say that women in prison are a lot more forthright than are men. They let it show when they're having a bad time, when they're struggling. For instance, a woman will straightforwardly say that she's an alcoholic. This kind of candor can be helpful, but it also requires a response. On a positive note, he talked about a woman in the institution who is thrilled to have two daughters graduating from Iowa State. Another woman is proud that her daughter is finishing high school, but feels horrible that she can't be there and be a mother to her daughter.

At the same time, some women fear leaving prison. They worry about how they will make contacts and where they will get support. This is where Witmer says that he draws upon The United Methodist Church system. He says, "I can call a UM church in just about any town in Iowa and set up a connection, a resource for a woman who upon release will be going there."

Witmer then spoke of the important practice of dealing with manipulation. "There is a lot of manipulation in this population. Of course there is; it's how you survive prison itself. And the manipulation can be very subtle." He hears a lot of sob stories, and some of them are true. But he cautioned that a prison pastor must be "as wise as serpents and as gentle as doves." He gave an example of a woman Whitmer had helped to find a very supportive group in a local church in Iowa when she got out of the penitentiary. But the church called Witmer because they felt like they were working harder than she was. On closer investigation, they found she was working several churches, getting support from each one without the others knowing it, rent from one, cash for groceries from another.

On the issue of manipulation, Witmer then told me that he is a recovering alcoholic and that attending Alcoholic Anonymous meetings are a necessary practice for him. He went on, "One of the things we say in AA is that you can't bullshit a bullshitter. But that's not quite true; actually, you can." He said, "I catch myself saying things that are not quite right, that are not quite the whole story." He then added, "The lens of trauma is not clear." He says that he hears a story from an inmate, and that he does not doubt her; he has compassion for her; he knows she's having a bad time. Yet he also knows that there is more to the story. There is a lot more to learn. Things are not crystal clear. First, he said, "I guess you need a hermeneutic of suspicion," but then he corrected himself by saying that he's not satisfied with the word ***suspicion***. Rather, he said, "I guess we need a hermeneutic of *there's more to the story*."

During the COVID crisis, Witmer found that weekends with other prison congregation pastors were important for coping. Comparing notes, commiserating, sharing feelings, prayer, and spiritual practices helped. He also noted that some clergy group meetings and conversations just don't translate into prison ministry. That's where he found his own spiritual contemplation important, not only to get through a tough time but to truly deepen and form his own life.

His own practices of contemplation have found receptivity in prison. One of these is breathing. He often begins worship with a breathing exercise. Along with this he uses silence and *lectio divina*. "Prisons are very noisy places," he explains. "And there's no room for silence. Sometimes you hear people getting in each other's faces; other times it's the sound of violence; sometimes it's like junior high school on a bad day." Recently, he used prayer stations around the room in worship, so that one could go to one station to engage art, another to receive Holy Communion, and yet another for anointing. Twenty minutes were given in the worship service for participation at these prayer stations. Further, he indicated that people in worship in the prison were not allowed to touch each other, but lately they have been given permission to hold hands in small circles of prayer.

Witmer allowed that "you hear a lot about being saved and converted in prison, and that's okay." But he believes that "spiritual practices take women further into healing and into transformation." He makes use of Thomas Keating's contemplative outreach and four guidelines of Centering Prayer.[54] Years ago, a Buddhist mediation teacher had begun a meditative group in prison, but it did not survive COVID. At the time, thirty-five women were coming to the chapel for twenty minutes of Centering Prayer five days a week. He also referred to the success story of Folsom Prison, which at one time was the most violent penitentiary in the US, with two hundred stabbings a year. The introduction of practices of meditation in Folsom Prison significantly reduced its violence.

Concluding our interview, Witmer named the importance of self-care in his personal life. He referred to the time of his active alcoholism after he had taken on the rigor of a new church start, gone through a divorce, and lost his job. Self-care following this hard time was simply lifesaving, he says. Today he has a spiritual director and sees a therapist. He swims, bikes, exercises, and is disciplined about observing the sabbath. It may not be Sunday, but he observes a sabbath rest one day out of seven.

To catch the full impact of the interview with Witmer, it may be necessary to read the above again, maybe twice. It is so full of small practices that one can miss them. Spiritual exercises of contemplation, breathing, *lectio divina*, the use of stations in worship, Centering Prayer, and more seem central to Witmer's life and to his justice ministry. The sensibilities and the savvy needed for pastoring in a women's prison require practices of compassion and a serpentine loss of innocence: genuine caring balanced with the capacity to recognize bullshit and manipulation, often at the same time with the same person; showing up and seeing purpose in lifeless, monotonous meetings added to the Sisyphean work of dealing with the vengeful Iowa legislature; pastoring and seeking silence amid the trauma and the noise of prison life; developing models of ministry that are collaborative and designed to empower; giving oneself over to exercises that can form and transform and give voice to inmates, sometimes against the objection of penal authorities; dealing day in and day out with women who want to be released to their children and yet panic at leaving the walls of an incarcerated existence; and, then, to struggling with your own addiction and seeking self-care. All these and more constitute a large collection of micro practices.

Doing Time

In chapter 2, I discussed the way James D. Tindall Sr. became a pastor to prisoners and used scripture at Leavenworth Federal Penitentiary, where he was incarcerated for three years. In this chapter, I want to fill out more of the story that shaped his prison experience and the range of practices he employed there while a prisoner.

First, I need to report more from our interview about his life and ministry prior to Leavenworth. Tindall says that he "came off 12th Street," a core city area of the Black community in Kansas City, Missouri, and that he grew up in the projects. He states that he can relate to people because he understands what it's like getting your lights turned off. He pastored a church for forty-two-and-a-half years in the Black community, and he's been in ministry for fifty-five years and is still working as a bishop. He has a sharp consciousness of the powers that be. For these reasons, among others, he says he can "mix with everybody."

As he worked in the community, the way he was treated negatively by the White community affected him, so he took personal action. Early on, he got involved with the NAACP, the Urban League, and other civil rights groups. He marched in protests and was active in welfare rights and other causes in the sixties and seventies. For fourteen years he worked as the religion director for a radio station, which got him involved in politics. In 1980 he was elected as a state representative. He notes that he did not have to raise money for his campaign because he was known in the community, and the cooperation of local volunteers helped him beat an incumbent opponent.

As a state representative, however, he had "an awakening in going to Jefferson City," the state capital and location of the legislature. He found the system to be overwhelming. It was impossible to get anything done because of the power of the majority Republican Party. Tindall feared that this political situation was such that he would have to tell the community that he had failed to make anything happen.

At that point, the community asked him if he would run for county legislature. He ran and won, and he served the county effectively for a total of twenty-one years. In this work, he found that the most important thing for ministry is to be involved with and understand the needs of the community. "If you work with the community, you know what their needs are." Criticizing some political leaders today who think they know but do not, he asserted, "You can't plan *for* the community. The community must be engaged." He complained specifically that a one-eighth cent sales tax in Kansas City tat was intended to provide ten to twelve million dollars a year for economic development in the Black community did not work because the board governing that expenditure did not listen to the needs of the people.

In his pastoral ministry he worked to address the social and political needs of the secular community as well as the religious. For example, Tindall emphasizes that city water, taxes, and a great many other things, come out of the political process. That's why he encourages his church and other denominations to be involved in all facets of politics affecting their lives.

Tindall interjected at this point that—regardless of a person's individual beliefs or lifestyle—he does not believe in condemnation, and that he has taught this to his congregation. One day a man came into his church who was clearly drunk. Sitting down in the back pew, he fell asleep. The congregation wanted to throw him out. But Tindall called the leadership together and said, "He's drunk, but he's where he ought to be." That did it, the man stayed and later went into recovery. "Ultimately, God did change him," Tindall reports.

The charges, the trial, and the conviction that led to Tindall's incarceration in Leavenworth Penitentiary occurred while he was chair of the Jackson County Legislature. He had had an ongoing disagreement with a judge in Kansas City who wanted funding for a new jail because the existing one was overcrowded. So, the judge summoned Tindall to his office, and they met once a week for three years.

Tindall's position was that it's not smart to build a new jail until you know who's going to be there. Tindall was asked to put a plan together for the jail and met every week with judges, the police department, bonding officials, prosecutors, and others. He found that the best step to reduce overcrowding was to release people on bond instead of putting people in jail for offenses like stealing hubcaps, not paying child support, and traffic tickets. He got agreement on this and took it to the judge to okay it, which he did. Within three weeks the jail went from a population of more than eight hundred to just over three hundred.

But the judge still insisted on building a new jail. When Tindall refused to go along, he was indicted on nineteen charges of bribery, embezzlement, and other improprieties. The case was originally assigned to another judge, but Tindall's judiciary opponent demanded that the case be reassigned to him, and he refused to recuse himself.

Tindall reports that all these were trumped-up charges. Not only that, but the prosecution showed a picture of him in handcuffs when he was much younger and made comments about his character. He didn't even know they had the pictures, but pictures of him in handcuffs were not unusual, as he had been arrested eighteen times during the civil rights struggle.

They also had a picture of Tindall and a woman who is a member of his church and the choir. Because she was active in the church, they sometimes traveled together to meetings. "The prosecution had taken pictures and tried to make it a romantic affair," Tindall reports. At the time of the trial, members of his congregation were sitting in the court room laughing at the very suggestion of an impropriety between the two of them. They knew that the lady was Tindall's best friend's wife. There was no affair.

Tindall revealed in our interview a concern he had had for some time. "I knew my life would either be taken or I would be locked up. I knew the time would come when they would 'find' something and that somebody would come after me."

The jury acquitted Tindall of all but one of the charges—federal tax fraud—understating his 1992 income, which should've been a misdemeanor. To this day, Tindall does not understand why it happened. Yet there was more; the judge overruled the jury and ordered a pre-sentence investigation and gave Tindall the maximum sentence of three years.

As Tindall prepared for prison, he was fearful. He did not know what would happen there. Even worse, he did not know what God was doing. He even said to himself, "Maybe I am a bad person, maybe I did do all those things."

On his last Sunday at the church before imprisonment, he told the congregation that he was leaving at ten o'clock the next morning. Church people lined up in their cars and followed him all the way to Leavenworth.

After their arrival at the penitentiary, the authorities would not let people come to the gate. So, Tindall stood there alone. He said in our interview, "That's a horrible feeling. Nothing but me and God. The loneliest time of my life. I saw men in chains. I could not imagine being in chains and shackles."

"But then relief came," he says. They gave him different clothes, khaki pants and shirt. They took him to the honor camp in a little bus wearing no shackles or handcuffs. When he arrived at the door of the honor camp, twenty inmates welcomed him. One man said to him, "Bishop, we need you to run a revival." And Tindall said to himself, "*I* need a revival."

Well, as Tindall entered the honor building, he encountered "Interstate" Bonticello (not his real name), a big-time gangster and enforcer from the mob in Kansas City who was serving a sentence.

Interstate greeted him warmly and said, "I got you taken care of, Bishop, don't worry about a thing." He had a shaving bag for Tindall with everything in it and told him, "You're not gonna be in a dorm. You've got a private room." Tindall told me, "Interstate took care of me. I even had luxury towels."

Tindall further informed me that some of the Black security guards attended his church and treated him with the highest respect. Tindall came to see in these events that the Lord was speaking to him. He also recalls that he got in an argument with God. He was crying, and God spoke to him, "Why are you crying? I have taken care of everything." From then on things became clearer and clearer.

"I wouldn't give anything for that experience," Tindall said. "It made me a better person. I learned a whole lot. I learned you can't trust everybody, but I have a lot of trust in the people."

He then went on to say that he felt sorry for so many of the young men in prison. For example, they had drug reduction classes that could take two years off your sentence if you took them. Most people of color in Leavenworth were in there for drugs, but the prison would not let Black men take the course, telling them they did not qualify. In one case, a White man served only two years of a much longer sentence. The warden, when pressed about the difference in the treatment of races, only said, "There's nothing we can do about this."

"There is work you can do in prison and get paid for it," Tindall went on, "but the hardest jobs get paid the least, and 90 percent of the good jobs went to Whites." The small amounts of money earned could be used in the commissary. Tindall, however, because of who he was, had no job. The prison authorities did not want him to go outside the walls because the news people might claim that he had no work and was being given special treatment. Yet he had plenty of money because at mail call he would typically get seventy-five to one hundred letters every day with money inside the envelopes. Guards, who got to know him and who saw how much public support he received said to Tindall, "You ought not to be here."

Without a prison job, Tindall knew that he had to come out of his pity party and began to speak about having "a positive mental attitude" to other inmates, which I reported earlier. He told them that they must not be circumscribed by their circumstances. "Inmates would receive 'Dear John' letters, and I had to deal with that," he said. He began a classroom ministry on Tuesday and Thursday evenings where he would provide sermons, positive support, and biblical studies. He held revivals. When he preached on Tuesday night at six o'clock, there was standing room only. The warden ordered that the cafeteria be opened to accommodate the crowd.

Through actions like these and those reported in chapter 2, Tindall became the informal pastor of the prison. He is a highly competent preacher who knows the Bible well. He also grew up in the core city and is existentially shaped by its poverty, its exclusion, its powerlessness, and its marginality. So Tindall had the credibility and skills to be the pastor of penitentiary life. After nearly three years of confinement, the prisoners wanted him to stay. Tindall told me that a lot of the men preaching today were former inmates who attended the revivals, and that inmates after their release joined Tindall's church and are still there.

As the time neared for his release, the prison planned a ceremony honoring Tindall. The warden came down to see him, and because it was Black History Month, Tindall asked if they could have an observance. The warden agreed to this proposal, and two prominent Black pastors were invited. Jesse L. Douglas of Detroit and Wallace Hartsfield of Kansas City came and preached.

When Tindall's prison sentence ended, Sam Mann, whom we met earlier in the book, came to take him home. Tindall says that "Sam was crying like a baby."

If you look back over the life and ministry of Tindall, it is stunning to think of the range of his work. Growing up in the projects of the core city, working in radio, being a state representative and a Jackson county legislator and chair, his engagement with the community and acquaintance with local needs, his sensibilities about the social and political process, his pastoral capabilities not only in his long experience as pastor of a local church but also in a prison and as an episcopal leader: every one of these ventures is filled with a host of practices too numerous to name. After he came home from Leavenworth, he was elected to two straight terms on the county legislature. He had to resign during the second term because of a law that forbade felons to serve in political office. The law had not been enforced until someone in a lesser office was required to resign, and with that a further complaint was registered against Tindall.

For more than twelve years, I have worked with Tindall in the Urban Summit, a major Black advocacy group in Kansas City. I have seen him initiate efforts because he has the kind of spiritual and moral authority to do so. He can connect and work with people from a wide variety of backgrounds because he has relational skills. He takes on issues because he has courage and is willing to move into controversy. His knowledge and capacity to act in the political arena are unsurpassed in our town. His unwillingness finally to condemn anyone makes him a defender of those who do not have a defense. His agility in a wide assortment of circumstances reveals not only carefully honed skills, but abiding and embodied theological commitments. He is a master of micro practices that have macro consequences.

CONCLUSION

I began these pages fully convinced of the importance of micro practices in justice ministry, so it does not surprise me that there must be several hundred named here, although I have not counted. I was surprised, however, that I found myself so moved by the witness of these pastors. I was inspired by the face-to-face liturgies, rituals, litanies, acts of etiquette, greetings, connections, and drills—yes, drills—of courtesy and kindness. I was stirred by the bonding and sustaining character of the gatherings I heard about, the moments of praise and recognition, the thoughtful yielding of center stage, and the acknowledgment of the silent and the sidelined. A justice of touch and a touch of justice provide alternatives to invasions and violations of the most sacred and intimate territories of selves and social bodies that are meant to live out an image of the divine and beloved communities.

So, drawing justice and community from the Bible, being moved and governed by it, mastering its use in prison and oral (and, yes, even in literate and digital) cultures, and living a theology that still works when things don't work out: these are the results of micro practices and the embodiment of an alternative society that can occur right under the nose of and in resistance to the principalities and powers.

Yet the stories, the practices, the competencies, and the skills of the clergy are not widely known. I am sure that they are mentors to others, but I came away concerned that so much of the work of the church around justice occurs in education but not in training. We have so many people who have ideas and positions on social issues but lack the craft and skills of doing justice that are so well-attested by the practitioners in our project.

It is like reading books and listening to instruction about baseball but never actually throwing, catching, and batting—never being in a game. All my life I wanted to go to Major League Baseball's spring training, so when we moved to Arizona, I went to the preseason games. They were terribly disappointing because the players were working on different parts of their skills. They were not so much playing baseball as trying out small changes, such as the way a pitcher gripped the ball or a batter changed his stance in the batter's box.

Then I discovered the training sites where the players did their routines in the morning. I remember my fascination watching eight pitchers take turns throwing an imaginary pitch from the mound to a coach at home plate who would then roll a ball down the first- or third-base line. Each pitcher would practice running to field the ball and throwing to first base. As I watched, I remembered pitching a ten-inning shutout in college and then, in the next inning, fielding a bunt and throwing the ball wildly past the first baseman into right field. My error cost us the game. Never in baseball practice sessions before had I fielded bunts and made repetitive throws to first base.

We need more people working as apprentices to clergy who are adept in justice ministry. Our seminars and workshops should be less devoted to lectures and discussions and more centered on training skills. I think, for example, of training people to do one-on-ones or the JustFaith Ministries where they use videos and then practice working with nonviolent language and peaceable interaction. I think of broad-based community organizing where people can work under the tutelage of well-versed organizers. The possibilities are endless.

And of course, the work of justice and the doing of change are reflected in this book by a range of different settings with pastors highly competent in different dimensions, settings, and populations. The contexts in these pages are urban, suburban, small town, and rural. And each requires its own substantive, concrete, and specific approach. But the crucial role of practices like biblical and theological grounding, relationship building, listening, and disciple leadership is clear in each setting.

I think also of practices that deal with failure so that one does not become mired in frustration and blame. There are alternative practices to the recitation of failure, and our clergy who spoke to it offer a dozen or more such exercises to turn loss into a different future. These acts of memory can be the commemoration of those who shaped and formed us. Indeed, they can stand like a great cloud of witnesses, but not only witnesses. They can be exemplars of skilled practices and alternative ways of being in the world.

Finally, we have seen in interview after interview the importance of becoming adroit in conflict, controversy, and confrontation. The micro practices of forceful, principled engagement take one out of the posture of passivity, avoidance, and fear-driven hesitation. Even jails and prisons have spaces for alternative practices that shape people to be alive even in that particular context.

Is an orientation to micro practices fail-safe? Of course not. These exercises embody, participate in, and indwell the intrinsic value of what is being done. If justice is being pursued, they are practices of justice. In opposition to oppression, they are practices of resistance—the weapons of the weak—and never has there been a totalitarianism that can ultimately overcome the concerted micro practices of the powerless, the excluded, the dominated, and the oppressed. Micro practices are the way we shape ourselves, our bodies, our passions, and our posture in the world. They infuse the gatherings where social acts make us one and where we find the formation, resolve, and transformation to do justice.

NOTES

1. Endesha Ida Mae Holland, *From the Mississippi Delta* (New York: Simon & Schuster, 1997), 263–272. This is an extraordinary book about a young woman who was a sex worker in Greenwood until she joined the SNCC organizing work there. Holland later earned a PhD and became a professor at the University of Southern California's School of Theater and its Gender Studies Program. She authored several plays, including *From the Mississippi Delta*, which ran off-Broadway at Circle in the Square and was nominated in 1988 for a Pulitzer Prize. Tragically, she died at 61 of complications of ataxia, a degenerative neurological condition.
2. For a good overview of the development of micro practices in sociology up until the mid-1980s, see Randall Collins, *Theoretical Sociology* (New York: Harcourt Brace Jovanovich, 1988), 375–409. See also Erving Goffman, *The Presentation of Self in Everyday Life* (New York: Doubleday, 1959); *Interaction Ritual* (New York: Doubleday, 1967); *Strategic Interaction* (Philadelphia: University of Pennsylvania Press, 1969); Harold Garfinkle, *Studies in Ethnomethodology* (Englewood Cliffs, NJ: Prentice Hall, 1967); Pierre

Bourdieu, *Outline of a Theory of Practice* (Cambridge: Cambridge University Press, 1977); *The Logic Of Practice* (Stanford, CA: Stanford University Press, 1980); and *Distinction: A Social Critique of the Judgment Of Taste*, trans. Richard Nice (Cambridge, MA: Harvard University Press, 1984). Among fairly recent popular accounts, see Matthew B. Crawford, *Shop Class As Soulcraft: An Inquiry into the Value Of Work* (New York: Penguin, 2009) and *The World Beyond Your Head: On Becoming an Individual in an Age of Distraction* (New York: Farrar, Straus and Giroux, 2015); B.J. Fogg, *Tiny Habits: The Small Changes That Change Everything* (Boston: Houghton Mifflin Harcourt, 2020). Among recent theological works, see James K. A. Smith, *Desiring the Kingdom: Worship, Worldview, and Cultural Formation* (Grand Rapids, MI: Baker, 2009); Craig Dykstra, *Growing in the Life of Faith: Education and Christian Practice*, 2d ed. (Louisville, KY: Westminster John Knox, 2005); Dorothy C. Bass and Craig Dykstra (eds.), *For Life Abundant: Practical Theology, Theological Education, and Christian Ministry* (Grand Rapids, MI: William B. Eerdmans, 2008). For works dealing especially with micro practices of resistance by those in lower class positions and other locations of marginality, see Michel de Certeau, *The Practice of Everyday Life,* trans. Steven Rendel (Berkeley, CA: University of California Press, 1984) and James C. Scott, *Weapons of the Weak: Everyday Forms of Peasant Resistance* (New Haven, CT: Yale University Press, 1985) and *Domination and the Arts of Resistance: Hidden Transcripts* (New Haven, CT: Yale University Press, 1990).

3. Karoline M. Lewis, *John: Fortress Biblical Preaching Commentaries* (Minneapolis: Fortress, 2014).

4. Regarding oral culture, the very best work I have seen on this is from Walter Ong. His books, *The Presence of the Word* (Minneapolis: University of Minnesota Press, 1967) and *Orality and Literacy* (New York: Routledge, 1982) are required reading for people who work with those of a secondary orality in a dominantly literate culture. I took the work of Ong and others and developed their applications for ministry. See my *Ministry in an Oral Culture: Living with Will Rogers, Uncle Remus, and Minnie Pearl* (Louisville, KY: Westminster John Knox Press, 1994). For an appreciative look at oral culture, see philosopher David Abram, *The Spell of the Sensuous* (New York: Vintage Books, 1996). His work with philosopher Maurice Merleau-Ponti opens up new vistas for understanding and recognizing the contributions of oral culture to our own time, especially the ecological/environmental challenge.
5. I am very much aware that we now live in a digital culture as well, one that takes form in digital literate and digital oral forms. I have given attention to these in a couple of books where I draw a sharp distinction between the "critical distance" of a literate culture and the "critical immersion" of a digital one. See my *The Spectacle of Worship in a Wired World* (Nashville, TN: Abingdon Press, 1998), 95–104; and *Powerful Persuasion* (Nashville, TN: Abingdon Press, 2005), 155–175.
6. This formulation accurately reflects Luther's metaphor in his *Preface to the Old Testament*, though he wasn't so succinct. He wrote that in the scriptures "you will find the swaddling cloths and the manger in which Christ lies, and to which the angel points the shepherds."

7. Eugene Peterson translates this passage as "The word became flesh and blood and moved into the neighborhood." See *The Message* (Colorado Springs, CO: NavPress Publishing Group, 1993), John 1:14. The Greek word here is *schenoo*, which means literally "to pitch tent." See also Samuel Wells, *Improvisation: The Drama of Christian Ethics* (Grand Rapids, MI: Brazos Press, 2004). To follow an incarnate Christ involves the development of theological chops.
8. John A. Lovelace, "Bubble Up Theology Revives Urban United Methodist Church," *The United Methodist Reporter* (October 14, 1988), 4.
9. Janet Wolf, *Practicing Resurrection: The Gospel of Mark and Radical Discipleship* (New York: United Methodist Women, 2019), 7–8 and 141–143.
10. Wolf, *Practicing Resurrection*, 7.
11. Wolf, *Practicing Resurrection*, 8.
12. Wolf, *Practicing Resurrection*, 11–12.
13. Wolf, *Practicing Resurrection*, 140–41.
14. Wolf, *Practicing Resurrection*, 142–43.
15. Wolf, *Practicing Resurrection*, 141–42.
16. See Eric Law, The Kaleidoscope Institute, https://www.kscopeinstitute.org for the principles for these two practices.
17. For elaboration of Rendle's point, browse his name and a good number of articles will appear as well as several of his more recent books.
18. Kathleen Norris, *The Quotidian Mysteries: Laundry, Liturgy and "Women's Work"* (Mahwah, NJ: Paulist Press, 1998).
19. https://faithinaction.org/

20. https://kounkuey.org/
21. https://www.hopics.org/
22. Counihan's discussion of neighborhood exegesis reminded me of William H. Poteat, *The Primacy of Persons and the Language of Culture* (Columbia, MO: University of Missouri Press, 1993), 51–55. Working with Ludwig Wittgenstein's notion of language games, Poteat names subsets of language games that I find very important: "Universes of discourse," "neighborhoods of speech," "familiar universe of discourse," "language regions," "logical neighborhoods," "linguistic topographies," "features of the linguistic landscape," "the environment of words," and "the landscape of our talk." I am now working with these notions attempting to think of linguistic breakdowns like locale, quarter, community, zone, "neck of the woods," linguistic neighborhoods, linguistic ghettos, linguistic parishes, linguistic precincts, or vicinity or field or enclave or neighborhood slang. It seems to me that ministry would be well served to understand the linguistic neighborhoods in which it takes place, a vital part of neighborhood exegesis.
23. Gustavo Gutiérrez, *A Theology of Liberation: History, Politics, and Salvation*, trans. and ed. by Sister Caridad Inda and John Eagleson (Maryknoll, NY: Orbis, 1973, 1988), 192–94 in 1973 edition and 108–10 in 1988.
24. Walter Wink wrote a trilogy on the powers, *Naming the Powers: The Language Of Power in the New Testament*; *Unmasking the Powers: The Invisible Forces that Determine Human Existence*; and *Engaging the Powers: Discernment and Resistance in a World Of Domination*, all published in Minneapolis by Fortress Press, 1984, 1986, and 1992, respectively. Wink also published *The Powers*

That Be: Theology for a New Millennium (New York: Doubleday, 1998), which he describes as "in large part a digest of the third volume of his trilogy, with elements from the previous two." This volume also draws from his book, *Violence and Non-Violence in South Africa* (Philadelphia: New Society, 1987).

25. On their website, COPS/METRO states that it "is a community-leader driven coalition of congregations, schools, non-profits, and unions working together to improve the conditions of families in San Antonio since 1974."
26. For a brief discussion of the cycle of organizing giving attention to each practice of that cycle, see my book, *A Christian Justice of the Common Good* (Nashville, TN: Abingdon Press, 2016), 96–106. For a more expansive treatment of broad-based community organizing in an international context, see Luke Bretherton, *Resurrecting Democracy* (New York: Cambridge University Press, 2015), chapters 1, 4, and 5.
27. Thomas C. Shelling, *The Strategy of Conflict* (Cambridge, MA: Harvard University Press, 1960) is a classic text. It is especially valuable for its discussion of threat. See the index for relevant pages. Also, the best short article I know that examines a range of tactics in bargaining and involves a lot of sanity about threats is that of George A. Brager and Valerie Jorrin, "Bargaining: A Method in Community Change," *Social Work*, Volume 14, Issue 4 (October 1969):73–83.
28. See the report of this study that relates it to complexity and chaos theory, Plowman, Stephanie Solansky, Tammy E. Beck, LaKami Baker, Mukta Kulkarni, and Deandra Villarreal Travis, "The Role of Leadership in Emergent, Self-Organization"

(University of Nebraska—Lincoln: DigitalCommons@University of Nebraska—Lincoln, 8.1.2007), 341–46. See also John Flowers and Karen Vannoy, *Not Just a One-Night Stand: Ministry with the Homeless* (Nashville, TN: Discipleship Resources, 2009).

29. I am supplementing some of the detail from Troxler's interview with an article he wrote about this experience, "Vecinos: A Good Samaritan Story," unpublished, provided by the author. Note that in this section on being with people, Troxler indicates his indebtedness to Samuel Wells, *A Nazareth Manifesto* (New York: Wiley, 2015).
30. Ed King and Trent Watts, *Ed King's Mississippi: Behind the Scenes of Freedom Summer* (Jackson: University Press of Mississippi, 2014), 7.
31. For a brief history of Medeiros's life, including his involvement with the farmworkers, see "Cardinal Humberto Medeiros: The Brownsville Years, 1966-1970," *The Pilot* (March 30, 2023), 1.
32. For reading about the failures and the excesses of corporate America that are doing so much damage to the bottom 40 percent of our class structure, to people of color, to women, to democracy, to the environment, and to our international relationships, see in a short list: Gary Dorrien, *Economy, Difference, Empire: Social Ethics for Social Justice* (New York: Columbia University Press, 2010); Wolfgang Streeck, *How Will Capitalism End? Essays on a Failing System* (New York: Verso Books, 2017); Naomi Klein, *This Changes Everything: Capitalism vs. the Climate* (New York: Simon & Schuster, 2015); J. Bradford DeLong, *Slouching Towards Utopia: An Economic History of the Twentieth Century* (New York: Basic Books, 2022); J. Michael Lind, *The New Class War:*

Saving Democracy from the Managerial Elite (New York: Portfolio/ Penguin, 2020).

33. See Howard Zinn, *The Twentieth Century: A People's History* (New York: HarperCollins, 2003), 359. Breeden was given the title of "Holy Clown" by Kurt Vonnegut for the action, which Bill termed "nonviolent guerrilla street theater." A documentary film, *The Times of a Sign,* was produced and broadcast by PBS on POV.
34. John Flowers and Karen Vannoy, *Not Just a One-Night Stand: Ministry with the Homeless* (Nashville, TN: Discipleship Resources, 2009), 73–75.
35. I am working here with both my interview with Garman and with an unpublished paper he provided entitled "GBCI Story 5–5–22."
36. Garman, "GBCI Story," 1.
37. Andrew Levison, *The White Working Class Today: Who They Are, How They Think and How Progressives Can Regain Their Support* (Washington, DC: Democratic Strategist Press, 2013).
38. Three of my books are especially relevant to these issues of cultural traditionalists: *Ministry in an Oral Culture: Living with Will Rogers, Uncle Remus, and Minnie Pearl* (Louisville, KY: Westminster John Knox Press, 1994); *Blue-Collar Resistance and the Politics of Jesus: Doing Ministry with Working Class Whites* (Nashville, TN: Abingdon Press, 2006); *Working Class Rage: A Field Guide to White Anger and Pain* (Nashville, TN: Abingdon Press, 2018).
39. https://paceebene.org/
40. These principles/practices come from a Fellowship of Reconciliation flyer entitled "Interfaith Approaches to Nonviolence and Peacemaking," provided to me by Stoneking.

41. Occupy was a "leaderless movement." To say someone was a leader within that context only indicates that they offered leadership for a moment but then returned to the general and equal population of the Occupy community.
42. https://justfaith.org/
43. https://www.bread.org/
44. https://momsdemandaction.org/
45. Basler, *History of Penn Avenue UMC*, an unpublished paper provided by Basler.
46. Basler, *History*, 2.
47. https://www.cjamm.org/exodushouse/
48. Nissan David Dubov, "Tzimtzum," *Chabad.org*. See https://www.chabad.org/library/article_cdo/aid/361884/jewish/Tzimtzum.htm.
49. In the quotations in this paragraph I have used Wolf's book, *Practicing Resurrection*, 16–18, to develop further comments she made in the interview on the three practices reported here. Her comments in this paragraph on three emancipated practices come from Dorothee Sölle, *The Silent Cry: Mysticism and Resistance* (Minneapolis: Fortress Press, 2001), 90–93.
50. https://www.myjewishlearning.com/article/dayenu-a-jewish-template-for-gratitude/
51. This definition from Gourevitch is from *We Wish to Inform You That Tomorrow We Will Be Killed with Our Families: Stories from Rwanda* (New York: Pick a Door, 1998), 48.
52. Wolf, *Practicing Resurrection*, xi.
53. As reported by the director at the Fresh Start Women's Center in the 5th Judicial District of Iowa, Angela Kairados.

54. Thomas Keating, *Centering Prayer* (Louisville, CO: Sounds True, 2009). Keating's four "R's" of centering prayer are: Resist no thought. Retain no thought. React to no thought. Return ever so gently to the sacred word.